William Shakespeare

Mitchell Lane
PUBLISHERS

P.O. Box 196
Hockessin, Delaware 19707

Poets and Playwrights

Carl Sandburg

Emily Dickinson

Langston Hughes

Tennessee Williams

William Shakespeare

William Shakespeare

Jim Whiting

Copyright © 2007 by Mitchell Lane Publishers, Inc. All rights reserved. No part of this book may be reproduced without written permission from the publisher. Printed and bound in the United States of America.

Printing   1   2   3   4   5   6   7   8   9

Library of Congress Cataloging-in-Publication Data
Whiting, Jim, 1943–
    William Shakespeare / by Jim Whiting
        p. cm. — (Poets and playwrights)
    Includes bibliographical references and index.
    ISBN 1-58415-426-8 (lib. bdg.)
    1. Shakespeare, William, 1564–1616—Juvenile literature. 2. Dramatists, English—
Early modern, 1500–1700—Biography—Juvenile Literature. I. Title. II. Series.
    PR2895.W46 2006
    822.3'3—dc22

                      2006006107
ISBN-13: 9781584154266

ABOUT THE AUTHOR: Jim Whiting has been a remarkably versatile and accomplished journalist, writer, editor, and photographer for more than 30 years. A voracious reader since early childhood, Mr. Whiting has written and edited about 200 nonfiction children's books. His subjects range from authors to zoologists and include contemporary pop icons and classical musicians, saints and scientists, emperors and explorers. Representative titles include *The Life and Times of Franz Liszt*, *The Life and Times of Julius Caesar*, *Charles Schulz*, *Charles Darwin and the Origin of the Species*, *Juan Ponce de Leon*, and *The Life and Times of John Adams*. He lives in Washington State with his wife and two teenage sons.

PHOTO CREDITS: Cover, pp. 1, 3: North Wind Picture Archives; p. 6: The Hermitage, St. Petersburg, Russia; p. 11: Blue Lantern Studio/Corbis; p. 16: Peter Bowater/Photo Researchers, Inc.; p. 20: North Wind Picture Archives; p. 30: Stefano Bianchetti/Corbis; p. 34: Swim Ink 2, LLC/Corbis; p. 41: Chris Andrews, Chris Andrews Publications/Corbis; p. 48: North Wind Picture Archives; p. 51: Fine Art Photographic Library/Corbis; p. 60: Adam Woolfitt/Corbis; pp. 70, 78: North Wind Picture Archives; p. 86: National Portrait Gallery, London; p. 92: Historical Picture Archive/Corbis.

PUBLISHER'S NOTE: This story is based on the author's extensive research, which he believes to be accurate. Documentation of such research is contained on page 106.

    The internet sites referenced herein were active as of the publication date. Due to the fleeting nature of some web sites, we cannot guarantee they will all be active when you are reading this book.

Contents

*For Your Information

Born in 1573, Sir Henry Danvers was an English nobleman. He became involved in a feud that helped inspire Shakespeare to write *Romeo and Juliet*. Danvers was a soldier who fought in many battles. The black spot near his left eye is a patch covering a battle wound. He was so proud of it, he insisted that the artist, Anthony van Dyck, include it when he painted this portrait in the late 1630s.

Chapter
1

A Story of Love and Death

Shortly before noon on October 4, 1594, an English nobleman named Sir Henry Long was enjoying a leisurely lunch at a tavern. He was laughing and joking with a group that included his brother, Sir Walter Long, a couple of local judges, and other important men. With platters of hearty food and large tankards of ale, it was the late-sixteenth-century version of a modern-day power lunch. The men weren't trying to make business deals with one another. The fact that they could spend so much time at lunch and eat so well showed how powerful they were. They owned big estates that generated substantial incomes. Their servants and field hands did all the work, leaving the Longs and the others with plenty of personal time.

While they were eating, a group of more than a dozen armed men burst into the tavern. The Longs' young neighbors, Sir Henry Danvers and Sir Charles Danvers, were at the head of the intruders. The Danvers and the Longs couldn't stand each other—their families had been feuding for at least a century. It's likely that no one could recall the original cause of the feud. By then, it didn't matter. The mutual hatred was part of each family's heritage.

Not long before, Sir John Danvers—Henry's and Charles's father and himself a judge—had sentenced one of Walter Long's servants to jail on a robbery charge. Long was outraged. He used his considerable influence to get the servant released. Judge Danvers wasn't happy. He struck again. This time he jailed Walter Long himself. Soon afterward, he sentenced another of Long's servants on a charge of murder. Since Long was in jail, he couldn't help the servant.

Like their predecessors, Walter and Henry weren't about to let an insult from the Danvers family go by without retaliation. They stirred up their servants and other followers to take action against their enemies. In a series of brawls, one Danvers servant died and another one was injured.

The Longs' thirst for revenge wasn't quenched when Judge Danvers died late in 1593. Charles, the oldest son, became the next target. According to noted author Anthony Burgess, "Henry [Long] wrote insulting letters to Sir Charles, calling him a liar, a fool, a puppy-dog, a mere boy, and promising that he would whip his bare arse [buttocks] with a rod."[1] As we might say today, Henry told Charles, "I'm going to kick your butt!"

Charles wasn't going to let himself be pushed around. He decided to retaliate against the insulting letters. He wanted to prove that he was more than a "mere boy." He knew where to find his foe. The Longs were regulars at the tavern.

The situation escalated from angry words to actions. Charles hit Henry Long with a truncheon, a short heavy club similar to a policeman's baton. Long was furious. He drew his sword and stabbed Charles, seriously wounding him. At that point, according to the Wiltshire County Coroner's report on the following day, "[Henry] Danvers voluntarily, feloniously, and of malice prepense, did discharge in and upon the said Long a certain engine called a dagge [a type of pistol], worth 6/8, charged with powder and bullet of lead, which Danvers had in his right hand, and inflict a mortal wound upon the upper part of the body of Long, under the left breast, of which he instantly died, and that immediately after the felony they all fled."[2]

The Danvers brothers were declared outlaws. They appealed to another neighbor for help. This was Henry Wriothesley, the Earl of Southampton. Like the Danverses, the Earl was also a young man. He could identify with Henry's rash action. He helped the brothers escape to France, where they would be safe.

The earl had another friend who had probably been a house guest during or near the time that this incident took place. This friend was a rising young poet and playwright. People in London were already talking about him. His name was William Shakespeare.

Shakespeare was always looking for new material. The story of a long-simmering feud finally breaking out into physical violence and murder intrigued him. Today these are often the themes of popular plays and movies. They were no less likely to lead to box office success in Shakespeare's time.

Shakespeare faced one problem that doesn't plague modern-day American screenwriters. He knew that he couldn't write about the experience directly because of a censoring law that Queen Elizabeth had passed in 1559. "The queen instructed her officers not to permit any 'interlude' [play] to be 'played wherein either matters of religion or of the governance of the estate of the commonweal shall be handled or treated,'" writes Shakespeare historian Stephen Greenblatt. "The censors were alert to anything that came too close to contemporary controversies. Moreover, the monarch and the ruling class were uneasy about being represented onstage, no matter how flattering the portrayal. By allowing such representations, they would in effect be ceding control of their own persons, and they feared that the theater would only succeed, as the queen put it, in 'making greatness familiar.'"[3]

In other words, members of the current English nobility were strictly off-limits to dramatists. Fortunately, a friend had just given Shakespeare a book about the history of the Italian city of Verona. Part of the book contained the description of a long-standing feud between two prominent Veronese families, the Montecchis and the Capellettis. Their feud had an even longer history than the one between the Danverses and the Longs. It dated back at least to the time of the poet Dante Alighieri at the start of the fourteenth century. Dante's famous epic poem *The Divine Comedy* contains the first mention of the two families.

This story probably reminded Shakespeare of a well-known story of his own era. It was a long poem called *The Tragicall Historye of Romeus and Juliet*, written by Arthur Brooke in 1562. The poem also mentioned the two feuding Veronese families.

Shakespeare may have already had the idea of updating Brooke's story. If so, the murder of Henry Long would have provided the ideal topical reference. The crime had received a lot of public attention. Most of the people who attended the play would have made the connection, but setting the story in Italy and using different characters with different names would avoid any problems with the royal censor.

It wouldn't have taken him long to write the play. Shakespeare had recently joined a new company of actors. They needed lots of plays—and they needed them quickly. Shakespeare had learned to write fast and well.

The result was *Romeo and Juliet,* one of Shakespeare's best-known plays. He doesn't waste any time telling his audience what they are about to see. The play opens with a prologue, in which a group of actors speaks directly to the audience:

Two households, both alike in dignity

In fair Verona, where we lay our scene

From ancient grudge breaks to new mutiny. (Prologue 1–3)

Right away the audience knows that the two households (Shakespeare slightly changes their names to Montague and Capulet) have long been enemies. The resentment is just as strong now as it has always been. A new "mutiny," or fight, is about to break out.

Shakespeare eliminates any element of suspense about the outcome of the play. A few lines later, we learn how it will end:

Do with their death bury their parents' strife.

The fearful passage of their death-mark'd love,

And the continuance of their parents' rage,

Which, but their children's end, nought could remove. (Prologue 8–11)

Shakespeare hammers home the point, mentioning their deaths three times in four lines. The two feuding families will be reconciled, and the reconciliation will cost them the lives of their children.

Shakespeare knew he had to grab the attention of the audience right away. As soon as the prologue ends, servants of the two rival houses begin quarreling. Within moments, the quarrel has escalated into open violence. All the characters pull out their swords and fall on their rivals. The clanging of steel on steel continues for several minutes. The fighting even includes the leaders of the respective families. In many productions, the swordplay claims a victim or two before a fragile peace can be restored.

Soon afterward, Romeo Montague and Juliet Capulet meet at a masked ball. They fall in love before they realize that the other one is a member of the hated family. The hatred doesn't matter to them. All they want is to be with each other. In the audience, we root for them, because they are so young (Romeo is fifteen and Juliet is thirteen) and in love. They are very appealing.

The hatred of their respective families is too great to overcome. Their plan to get out from beneath its crushing weight goes tragically awry. Both of them die. As the play concludes, one character says,

In the tragic final scene of *Romeo and Juliet,* Romeo believes that Juliet is dead. Unwilling to live without her, he commits suicide by taking poison. But Juliet has faked her death. When she wakes, she sees the poison container that Romeo has just emptied and realizes he is dead. She stabs herself with his dagger and dies.

For never was a story of more woe
Than this of Juliet and her Romeo. (V. iii. 310–311)

Romeo and Juliet is probably the best-known of Shakespeare's plays among young people. Romeo and Juliet are typical of teenagers who want to be with someone who does not meet their parents' approval. They have to sneak out of the house to see each other. We clearly see how much they love each other. Moviemakers aren't blind to this attraction. A number of films that either follow the play literally or transfer it to a modern setting have been huge box-office favorites.

Many of the lines from *Romeo and Juliet* are familiar even to people who haven't seen or read the play:

A pair of star-cross'd lovers (Prologue, 6)

But, soft! what light through yonder window breaks? / It is the east, and Juliet is the sun! (II. ii. 1–2)

O Romeo, Romeo! wherefore art thou, Romeo? (II. ii. 33)

What's in a name? that which we call a rose / By any other name would smell as sweet. (II. ii. 43–44)

Good night, good night! parting is such sweet sorrow. (II. ii. 84)

For Shakespeare, *Romeo and Juliet* was just a warm-up. In all, he would create nearly forty plays that have convinced many people he is the world's greatest writer. After he died, one of his fellow playwrights said, "He was not of an age, but for all time."[4]

One measure of his greatness is the vast number of words that he introduced into the English language. Many words and phrases taken from his plays are still in everyday usage. Few English-speaking people go through a day without paying unconscious homage to Shakespeare by uttering something that can be traced back to him. He even invented the popular knock-knock joke.

Another measure is the insights that he showed into human nature. Probably more so than any other writer, he dealt convincingly with emotions that everyone feels—love, hate, anger, laughter, despair, joy, and many more.

A third measure comes from a comparison with a book that was published during his lifetime, the King James Bible. This translation of the Bible may have been the best-selling book of all time, yet in many churches it has been supplanted by newer translations. These versions are written in updated English—language that is easier for most people to understand. By contrast, hardly anyone would dream of changing the language that Shakespeare uses.

A fourth is that his plays remain successful at the box office even though their author has been dead for nearly four centuries. Every year millions of people attend productions of Shakespeare's plays. Although they might not catch every word, they are just as moved as his contemporaries were.

Seven years after his death in 1616, two of his friends—Henry Condell and John Heminges—collected most of his plays and published them in book form. In their preface, the two men wrote, "Read him, therefore, and again, and again."[5]

That advice is just as true today as it was nearly four centuries ago.

A Man of Many Words

Knock Knock!

Who's there?

Who.

Who, who?

You don't who, owls do!

Knock knock jokes all have the same great-granddaddy: a grumpy doorman in Shakespeare's play *Macbeth*. He is fast asleep near the entrance of Macbeth's castle. Someone pounds on the door. As he rubs the sleep from his eyes and shuffles toward the door, he mumbles, "Knock! Knock! Who's there?"

This popular form of humor is just one of Shakespeare's many contributions to the English language. He is also credited with hundreds of everyday words. Shakespeare didn't necessarily invent them, but they appear in print for the first time in his plays and poems. These household words run from A (*anchovy*) to Z (*zany*) and include *bloodsucking, catlike, cold-blooded, eyeball, fairyland, fortune-teller, grime, grovel, hunchbacked, juiced, obscene, posture, puke, puppy-dog, tardiness, torture, unreal, watchdog,* and *worn-out*.

He also invented many common phrases, such as *fair play, for goodness' sake, good riddance, the milk of human kindness, neither a borrower nor a lender be, neither rhyme nor reason, a sorry sight,* and *a wild-goose chase*.

Many authors have used phrases taken directly from Shakespeare as the titles of their works. Ray Bradbury wrote *Something Wicked This Way Comes*. William Faulkner's *The Sound and the Fury* helped him win the Nobel Prize for Literature in 1949. *The Winter of Our Discontent* did the same for John Steinbeck thirteen years later.

Shakespeare was even a master of the put-down. "I would thou didst itch from head to foot: and I had the scratching of thee, I would make thee the loathsomest scab in Greece" (*Troilus and Cressida,* II. i. 27–29) and "mad mustachio purple-hued maltworms" (*Henry IV, Part 1,* II. i. 74–75) are typical of insults that his characters hurl at one another.

Scholars believe that no single individual has had a greater impact on the English language. That is saying a great deal. English has a long history. Its words come from many different sources.

For centuries surrounding the birth of Jesus of Nazareth, the inhabitants of the British Isles spoke Celtic (KEL-tik). While Celtic has largely disappeared, words such as *bucket, cart, noggin,* and *slogan* remain.

Beginning in the sixth century, warlike tribes from northern Germany came to Britain. One tribe, the Angles, spoke a language known as Angle-ish. The spelling eventually changed to *English*. Many common words date from that era. For example, the first line of the Lord's Prayer in "Old English" is *"Fæder ure, thu the eart on heofunum"* (Father our, thou that art in heaven).

In 1066, a French army led by William the Conqueror invaded England, defeated the English, and began ruling the country. French became the language of educated people; commoners spoke English. The two groups used different words to refer to the same food item. The French ate *beef* and *mutton*, while the English ate *cow* and *sheep*. Many words relating to law and government, such as *jury*, *verdict*, *county*, and *city*, were introduced. Eventually the two languages merged into "Middle English." The original English word often was more common than its French equivalent. A drowning person yells *"Help!"* instead of *"Aid me!"*

At the start of the Renaissance in the 1400s, Latin and Greek words found their way to England. Many, such as *pneumonia* and *chemistry*, reflected the increase of medical and scientific knowledge. Others, such as *chorus*, dealt with music.

The growth and expansion of the British Empire added native words from countries that fell under British control. For example, the words *shampoo* and *pajamas* originated in India. Further advances in science and medicine created the need for more new words derived from Latin and Greek roots, such as *oxygen, protein, nuclear,* and *vaccine.*

American English added many more, both from Native Americans and from early settlers of various nationalities. *Raccoon, tomato, canoe, barbecue, armadillo, ranch, Cajun, goober,* and *gumbo* are just a few of these words.

Many modern English words have roots in the languages of Native Americans.

The result of all these sources of input is that English is probably the most flexible and useful of all languages. It continues to grow and evolve. *Byte, cyber, hard-drive,* and *microchip* are examples of recent additions.

15

The Shakespeare Hotel is one of the oldest hotels in Stratford. It was established in 1637 when three separate houses were joined together. Each of its rooms is named for a character in one of Shakespeare's plays.

A Boyhood in the Countryside

William Shakespeare's birthplace was Stratford-upon-Avon, England, a small town about 100 miles northwest of London. At that time, the population was about 1,500 people.

We don't know exactly when Shakespeare was born. The most commonly accepted date is April 23, 1564. By law, children had to be baptized within five days of the day they were born. His baptism took place on April 26, 1564.

There was a practical reason for baptizing children so quickly. Infant mortality was very common. In that era, nearly everyone believed that only baptized people could go to heaven. Parents wanted to make sure that their babies would go to heaven even if they died within a few days. They hurried to church as soon as they could for this all-important ceremony.

The document listing his baptism is still on display in Stratford's Holy Trinity Church. Written in Latin, it identifies him as *Guiliamus filius Johannes Shakspere.* The English translation is "William son of John Shakspere."

It is one of just a relative handful of official documents that exist with specific information about the events of William Shakespeare's life. If we go by these documents alone, his life story wouldn't be very long. Yet many biographies about the man, most of them hundreds of pages long, have been written. How is this possible?

One reason is that we know a great deal about the era in which he lived. For example, we know the basic structure of the educational system that existed at that time. There is little reason to doubt that it was the type of education young William received.

For another, we know approximately when each of his plays was produced for the first time. This knowledge helps to trace the development of his writing ability and the way in which his plays show what was going on in his personal life.

For a third, his contemporaries had plenty to say about him while he was still alive. As biographer Peter Quennell observes, "From the year 1592, when he was attacked by an unhappy fellow poet, we find constant references to his increasing reputation as a writer, accompanied by numerous allusions to his human qualities. If these allusions are separately examined, we may find it difficult to draw a detailed portrait; but, if what we know of Shakespeare himself is combined both with the evidence that his work affords us and with our knowledge of his social period, a recognizable impression very soon emerges."[1]

As a result, it is possible to write a biography with a reasonable degree of certainty about the events of his life. Since Shakespeare lived and died so long ago, though, we don't have any way of knowing for certain if the educated guesses that biographers make about him are correct. Different biographers disagree about certain elements of his life. It's likely that these disagreements will never be resolved with certainty. However, there is general agreement about most of the important events.

One point of general agreement involves Shakespeare's ancestry. Stratford was located in Warwickshire. The word *shire* means "county," so we know that he was born in Warwick County. Shire records enable scholars to trace Shakespeare's ancestors back to at least the thirteenth century. At that time, there was a great variety of spellings of his name: *Chapsper, Choxper, Schaftspere, Shagspere, Shaxper, Shogspar,* and dozens more.

John Shakespeare, his father, was born into a farming family in 1530. An ambitious man, he quickly lost interest in being a farmer. He wanted a better life for himself and his family. There was a great demand for well-made gloves, so he became a glover.

Because mutton, the meat of sheep, was a popular part of people's diets, many sheep were slaughtered. The butchers had no use for the skins, so they would happily sell them to John Shakespeare. He used the skin to make his gloves. He also sheared the wool and sold it to weavers. By every indication, he became prosperous by the time he was in his late twenties. It was time to get married.

His wedding to Mary Arden probably took place in 1557. Mary's family owned a substantial amount of land in Warwickshire. Some scholars believe that his mother's background made her one of a relatively few women in that era who could read and write.

Biographer Park Honan notes, "From such evidence as exists and from genetic probability, she emerges as an intelligent, quick-minded, eager, and selfless person of use to generations of males, since it is likely that she had helped her father, husband, and eldest son in turn."[2]

The bond between mother and eldest son seems to have been especially close. One of Shakespeare's main strengths in his future career was portraying strong and sympathetic female characters. Perhaps his closeness to his mother gave him his exceptional insight into the female mind and emotional makeup.

The newlyweds settled in Stratford and purchased a large house on Henley Street. Now known as the Birthplace Museum, it is a popular tourist attraction. The rooms have been restored to appear the same as they would have when Shakespeare lived there. As was common in the times, the glove shop that John Shakespeare owned and operated was located in the house.

William was the oldest of six children. Two girls had preceded him, but they both died in infancy. William was fortunate that he didn't follow them. He was born during one of the plagues that often ravaged the English countryside. His five siblings were Gilbert (born 1566), Joan (1569), Anne (1571), Richard (1574), and Edmund (1580).

William was born into a very confused era. In 1517, a German clergyman named Martin Luther had begun the Protestant Reformation. The changes he inspired in organized religion created a great deal of chaos and uncertainty throughout Europe.

At first, the English King Henry VIII, whose reign had begun in 1509 when he was just eighteen, resisted Luther's ideas. England remained Catholic. In 1521, Pope Leo X praised the king, calling Henry the "defender of the faith."

Soon after he became king, Henry married a Spanish princess named Catherine. One of the purposes of the marriage was to strengthen the ties between England and Spain. Henry and Catherine had a daughter, Mary, in 1516.

Henry, who desperately wanted a male heir to succeed him, became increasingly disappointed with Catherine. She continued to "fail" him because she didn't bear him a son, or even more daughters. She had a series of miscarriages and stillbirths.

Eventually Henry fell in love with a young English noblewoman named Anne Boleyn. He believed that Anne would bear him a boy. He wanted to divorce Catherine and marry Anne. At that time, divorce was forbidden by the Church. Henry appealed directly to the Pope to make an exception for him. The Pope refused Henry's request.

Henry decided that if the existing church wouldn't allow him to be divorced, he would start his own. Eventually it became known as the Anglican Church, or the Church of England. In many rituals, it was definitely Protestant. Most importantly, it would allow Henry to divorce Catherine.

The birth of the new church created a major dilemma. Although many Englishmen were willing to join it, a number of English Catholics believed devoutly in their faith. They refused to change. Some were put to death for their beliefs. Others tried to conceal the fact that they remained Catholic. The strains seriously weakened the country.

English King Henry VIII (in red) met Anne Boleyn in 1527. Henry, who was married at the time, fell in love with her. After changing church laws, he was granted a divorce and married Anne six years later. Their child became Elizabeth I, one of England's most important rulers.

Henry married Anne Boleyn in 1533. When it came to producing male children, Anne was no more successful than Catherine. She did have a child—a daughter, Elizabeth. Not long afterward, Henry became convinced that Anne was cheating on him. Enraged, he ordered her execution in 1536.

He remarried eleven days later. His new wife was Jane Seymour. Jane quickly gave him a son, Edward, then died two weeks later. Edward proved to be a sickly boy. His long-term prospects for survival were not very good.

Henry married three more times. The fourth marriage, to Anne of Cleves, ended in divorce after less than six months. The fifth, to Catherine Howard, resulted in her execution. His final wife, Catherine Parr, outlived him. None of the three women produced any children.

Henry died in 1547. Between that year and Shakespeare's birth, England had four different monarchs: Edward, who died at the age of sixteen in 1553; the bizarre nine-day "reign" of teen queen Lady Jane Grey; Mary; and finally Elizabeth.

When Mary assumed the throne, she reinstated Catholicism as the country's official religion. Under her orders, hundreds of Protestants were burned at the stake. When she died in 1558, Elizabeth succeeded her and restored the Church of England. She also cracked down on Catholics, though she wasn't as violent as her half sister had been. Even so, religious turmoil continued to seethe beneath the surface.

Both of William Shakespeare's parents were descended from Catholics, but that didn't seem to hamper John's accomplishments. He became steadily more important in Stratford. About the time of his marriage, he broke into public life as the civic ale-taster. In that position, he was responsible for maintaining the quality of bread and ale, two of the dietary staples of the era. In 1559, he became petty constable, then continued his rise in importance with appointments as borough chamberlain and alderman. His ascent was complete in 1568 with his election as bailiff of Stratford, a position similar to a modern-day mayor. As bailiff, he could lay claim to being a "gentleman." Many gentlemen had coats of arms. John Shakespeare wanted one as well. His application was turned down.

Despite the setback involving the coat of arms, it is likely that his father's election as bailiff affected William as well. It would mark his father as an important man. "As an impressionable four-year-old, the future playwright would now see a clutch of mace-bearing sergeants arrive at Henley Street early each day to escort his fur-trimmed father, with great ceremony, in a procession through the streets of

Stratford to preside over the morning meetings at the Guild Hall,"[3] writes biographer Anthony Holden. It would have been the boy's first view of the royal courts that appear so often in his work.

One of John Shakespeare's responsibilities was determining what plays the people in Stratford could see. Groups of traveling players, or actors, regularly traveled through the countryside. When they came to a new town, they would present their plays in front of the bailiff. If the bailiff liked what he saw, he would give the players a license to perform. In 1569, two of these troupes visited Stratford. We don't know if John took his son to see the performances. If he did, it would mark William's introduction to the theater.

William's introduction to education probably came a few years later, when he was seven. It's likely that he began attending a local "petty school." The primary purpose of such schools was to teach students to read and write the English language. Perhaps they also learned some basic arithmetic. It was especially important for them to know the Catechism, which consisted of a series of questions and answers that summarized the basic beliefs of the Church of England. Stratford's petty school may have been among the best of its kind in all of England. A number of wealthy citizens had made generous donations to support it.

William would have learned how to use a hornbook, a flat slab of wood with a handle. It contained the letters of the alphabet and a copy of the Lord's Prayer. There was also a pronunciation guide to the vowels. The writing was protected by a very thin, transparent layer of cow's horn, which gave the hornbook its name.

Two years later, William would have entered the King's New School. In theory, attending school was free, but schools didn't provide much for their students except books. Families had to buy the students' supplies, such as writing instruments. In days before pens and pencils, the boys used quills dipped in ink. The quills had to be continually sharpened, so a penknife was also part of every student's daily equipment.

Writing paper was still another expense. Students were required to keep "commonplace books." These were notebooks in which they jotted down passages from the books they read that they thought could be of use to them in later life. England didn't produce very much paper. It had to be imported, which added to its price and made school attendance even more costly.

The cost of supplies kept some boys from attending school. Many others simply couldn't afford the time. They were needed to help out, either in the family business if they lived in town or with the chores if they lived on the farms in the countryside.

John Shakespeare didn't face these problems. There is every reason to believe that William had the opportunity to attend school.

He was fortunate. Like Stratford's petty school, the King's New School had a good reputation. All the teachers had university degrees.

The "New" in the school's name referred to King Edward VI, the short-lived son of King Henry VIII. For many years, English schools had been under church authority. The religious turmoil that began during the reign of Henry VIII changed that situation. Henry confiscated much of the church property. The schools were allowed to continue, but they were re-founded under the authority of the king. The one in Stratford was the last "King's New School." Just a few days after it had been reestablished, the frail Edward was dead.

Students were expected to be at school by 6:00 A.M. for prayer every day except Sunday. The boys studied for five hours, then had two hours off for lunch and recreation. Lessons resumed at 1:00 and continued until 5:00. Because of the decreased light in winter, school began at 7:00 A.M. and ended at 4:00.

The school was located on the upper level of the 150-year-old Stratford guildhall. Students sat across from each other at stretch versions of modern-day picnic tables. The master sat at a large elevated desk at one end of the room. A fireplace offered some heat, while windows and candles provided illumination.

The days were largely similar, though there were some variations. On Mondays the boys would spend part of the morning discussing the previous day's sermon. It was a given that they had attended church and were familiar with what the pastor had said. Thursday probably would have been the boys' favorite day: It was a "half holiday." In today's terms, we would call it early dismissal. They had the afternoon off. Friday was typically broken up by punishment of the week's offenders.

The schoolmasters used birch rods to punish unruly students and apparently beat their students for any infractions of the rules. Swearing was the most common violation. Other offenses included fighting, lying, playing cards, gambling with dice, and stealing. Even sneaking into nearby orchards and plucking apples off trees could occasion a couple of whacks.

In addition to the birch rods, many masters employed the ferule. The ferule's handle was a flat piece of wood. The "business end" was a larger wooden circle. Sometimes holes were drilled in the circle. These holes raised blisters on the rear end of the student being disciplined.

The masters undoubtedly believed that they were doing students a favor by paddling them. As author Anthony Burgess points out, "It was generally acknowledged among Elizabethan educationists that children had to have knowledge crammed, and sometimes beaten, into them."[4]

In Shakespeare's plays, schoolmasters usually were unsympathetic characters. These negative portrayals may suggest that he was frequently at the receiving end of blows.

Going to school wasn't very stimulating. Students weren't encouraged to think for themselves. The instruction was based on principles that had been established many years previously. Most scholars of that era believed that almost everything worth learning had been written many centuries before by the Greeks and the Latin-speaking Romans. While a few English translations of these classic works were available, it was believed that the best way of learning them was to read them in their original languages. One mark of an educated man was the ability to flawlessly recite long passages in Greek or Latin. Accordingly, the boys spent much of each day memorizing these passages. Sometimes they were punished if they spoke English.

They also received some instruction in mathematics. Religion was important as well. The students would have been instructed in the beliefs of the Church of England.

That was about it. Many subjects that today are considered essential weren't even considered. There was no history, no science.

William's first year at school probably focused on learning the eight parts of speech, with particular emphasis on memorizing many Latin nouns and verbs. In the second year, the boys would use this knowledge to construct sentences in Latin. Third-year students would focus on making translations from Latin to English and from English to Latin. To make their assignments even more difficult, sometimes the master would have the students translate a Latin passage into English. Several months later, he would have the students translate it back into Latin—without letting them see the original passage.

Older students would begin reading classical authors—in the original language, of course. Always there would be endless exercises in memorization. Shakespeare eventually made good use of this reading. One of the most important books that students read was Ovid's *Metamorphoses*. The book provided Shakespeare with a number of ideas that he would use later. For example, one of his earliest published works was a long poem called *Venus and Adonis*. It was very popular and helped to establish his reputation. The story came directly from Ovid.

In later life, he would be greatly influenced by Lord North's translation of Plutarch's *Lives*. Plutarch was an ancient author who wrote about notable Greeks and Romans. Some of Shakespeare's plays, such as *Julius Caesar* and *Antony and Cleopatra*, featured these characters. As he wrote, he probably had North's book sitting in front of him. Some of the language in the plays is remarkably similar to the original source.

At the end of each term, older students would perform the plays they had read during the previous few months. This practice almost certainly influenced Shakespeare. One of his earliest plays is *The Comedy of Errors*, which describes humorous situations involving two sets of identical twins. The plot comes from a play called *Menaechmi*, written by the Roman playwright Plautus. Perhaps William had a major role in the school production.

We don't know what William thought of going to school. In *As You Like It*, he wrote about "the whining school boy with his satchel / and shining morning face creeping like snail / unwillingly to school." (II. vii. 144–46) If he wasn't describing himself, he was certainly describing some of his classmates—as well as many schoolboys (and schoolgirls) even today in their reluctance to attend classes.

The students did have some time to enjoy themselves. They played an early version of cricket. Another popular game was a form of handball, in which the boys took turns hitting the ball off the school walls with their hands.

William may have had a somewhat extended break from his studies in 1575. Queen Elizabeth visited Kenilworth Castle, a few miles from Stratford. The castle was at the center of the extensive lands owned by the Earl of Leicester (pronounced LESS-tur). At periodic intervals, English monarchs made tours through their realm to show themselves to the people. Such a tour, which probably lasted for at least several weeks, was called a progress.

Progresses were especially important for Elizabeth. Her authority was shaky. There were still many Catholics in England. Catholic Spain was also becoming more and more belligerent. Elizabeth knew she had to make sure the country remained loyal to her. Her progresses increased her popularity and made her seem more legitimate.

During her visit to Kenilworth, the earl provided almost nonstop entertainment for her, including musical performances and plays. As bailiff of Stratford, John Shakespeare was important enough to receive an invitation to attend the festivities. If he did, he probably brought his oldest child with him. William was now eleven and old enough to understand what was going on. By this time he had probably participated in some of his school plays. It is hard to imagine him not wanting to see how plays were staged professionally.

One result of Elizabeth's rule was to create an atmosphere in which drama could thrive. She was not only one of the strongest women in history, she was one of the most cultured. She especially enjoyed watching plays. While she was very religious, she also encouraged the production of secular plays based on the classics.

It was customary for great men such as the earl to employ a troupe of actors to entertain on a regular basis. In fact, the Earl of Leicester's Men had done several performances in Stratford two years earlier. John Shakespeare almost certainly would have attended and been given preferential seating. He may have brought William with him.

The year of the progress seems to have marked the high point of John Shakespeare's life. His fortunes—and those of his family—declined shortly afterward. The following year he attended what would be his last town council meeting for many years. Apparently he owed large sums of money to various creditors. He had to sell part of the land that belonged to his wife. Religious factors may also have played a part in his decline. With the increasing emphasis on enforcing conformity to the Church of England, John Shakespeare may have wanted to maintain a very low profile because of his Catholic background. Avoiding public appearances would have been a logical way of achieving that goal.

With the family's finances and reputation in a downward spiral, William probably had to drop out of school not long afterward. Just entering his teenage years, William may have been affected in an especially personal way. Other boys his age may have mocked him because of father's decline. What must have been especially unhappy memories seem to have emerged in some of his plays.

As author Peter Ackroyd points out, "The plays of Shakespeare are filled with authoritative males who have failed. . . . Many of the central male characters of his drama have been disappointed in the practical business of the world. . . . This failure does not engender aggression or bitterness; quite the contrary. It is invariably the case that Shakespeare sympathises with failure."[5]

It's not clear what the young man did for the next few years. He probably helped his father make gloves. It's likely that his father also did some butcher work as a sideline. If so, William would have worked alongside him. His plays are dotted with precise references to the craft of being a butcher. He may have served as a private tutor. Some people speculate that he worked as a clerk in a law office. Perhaps he even left town for an extended period.

These are all educated guesses. There are no references to Shakespeare as a boy or for nearly all of his teenage years in any of the existing records from that time.

That situation changed suddenly and dramatically in the late fall of 1582. His name appears for two successive days in the parish register. The momentous occasion would catapult him into adulthood.

A Time of Royal Turmoil

When Edward VI died without leaving any direct heirs, England was left in a very unusual situation. All of Edward's potential successors were women. England had had only one previous female ruler. Matilda, also known as Maud, occupied the throne for two brief periods in the twelfth century. Both times she was overthrown. The conclusion seems obvious: English men didn't like to be ruled by women.

Besides their gender, the three most obvious choices to succeed Edward all had other disadvantages. Of Henry's other children, the oldest, Mary, would normally have been at the head of the line. However, she was a Catholic. She had also been declared illegitimate in 1532 in the controversy surrounding Henry's efforts to divorce Catherine and marry Anne Boleyn. Elizabeth would have been up next. She was Protestant, but with her mother's execution, she was reclassified as illegitimate four years after her older half sister.

With these problems in Henry's direct line, the succession went through his oldest sister, Margaret. Margaret had a daughter named Mary, who came with even more baggage. Margaret had married the king of Scotland. That made Mary a foreigner and eventually earned her the famous nickname of Mary Queen of Scots. On top of that, Mary was also a Catholic.

That left the teenaged Lady Jane Grey.

In an era that emphasized intermarriage among ruling houses for dynastic purposes rather than marriage for love, Lady Jane was unique. Henry VIII was especially fond of his youngest sister, Mary. He wanted her to marry the elderly king of France, but Mary was deeply in love with the Earl of Suffolk. The earl was Henry's best friend. Henry was angry about the earl's relationship with his sister. He considered it somewhat of a betrayal, but he found it hard to say no to Mary. Brother and sister cut a deal. Mary would marry the French king. When he died, she could marry the earl.

Mary lucked out in a way. The king of France died less than three months after the marriage. Henry kept his word. He let Mary marry the Earl of Suffolk. They had a son, who died in his teens. Their daughter Frances married an important nobleman named Henry Grey. Jane was the Greys' first child. Her descent from Mary, the sister of Henry, made her a legitimate heir to the throne.

John Dudley, the Duke of Northumberland, was the chief adviser to the young King Edward, which gave him a great deal of power. Dudley knew that

Noted scholar Roger Ascham visits the teenage Lady Jane Grey.

Edward was likely to die soon. He wanted to hang on to his powerful position. He thought he knew how. Dudley talked Edward into naming Jane as his heir. Then Dudley married her to his son Guilford on May 25, 1553. Lady Jane was sixteen at the time, and Guilford was only a year older. They barely knew each other when they married.

Edward died on July 6, 1553. Four days later Jane was proclaimed queen. She had almost no support outside the Dudley family and their friends. Jane didn't even want to be queen. She thought that Henry's eldest daughter, Mary, should become the new queen.

Many people supported Mary's claim. On July 19, she arrived in London and was immediately named queen. Jane just wanted to go home. She never did. She and her husband were imprisoned and executed early the following year.

Mary wanted to return England to Catholicism. She began burning Protestants. She quickly acquired the name of "Bloody Mary" for all the killing carried out during her reign. Elizabeth was fortunate that she wasn't among the victims.

Like her half brother Edward, Mary was somewhat sickly. Even though she was married, she was unable to bear an heir. When she died in 1558, Elizabeth succeeded her and immediately restored Protestantism. While she not as oppressive as her sister had been, it was clearly not a good time to be a Catholic.

Elizabeth knew that many people didn't approve of her. She didn't feel very secure. Her relative, Mary Queen of Scots, began to cast an envious eye on the throne. Elizabeth captured her and kept her imprisoned for many years. In 1587 Elizabeth ordered Mary's execution, removing the final major threat to her authority. Nonetheless, her secret police were always active, looking for evidence of other conspiracies against her. They had plenty of work to do.

The lavish room in which Shakespeare stands suggests that he is in a nobleman's home. The home probably belongs to the Earl of Southampton, Shakespeare's early patron.

Chapter 3

Love and Marriage

On November 27, 1582, the Stratford parish register notes William Shakespeare for the first time since his birth. This time it records the granting of a marriage license to William Shaxpere and Anna Whateley. The following day, a license is granted to William Shagspere and Anne Hathwey. Most scholars assume that the slight differences in the spelling of the names of the bride and groom aren't significant. They believe that the entries refer to the same two people.

In addition to the apparent redundancy of the second entry, there are several unusual aspects to this license. For one thing, Shakespeare was only eighteen. It was very uncommon for young men to be married at that age. Typically, Elizabethan men would wait until their late twenties. By then they were firmly established in their trade and could support a family. In fact, William wasn't even old enough to make the decision to get married on his own. He needed the permission of his parents. His bride-to-be, Anne Hathaway (the commonly accepted spelling of her name), was twenty-six, several years older than the customary age of marriage for women. It was also customary for Elizabethan husbands to be older than their wives.

There were other interesting elements. The second entry includes a guarantee from two well-to-do local farmers, Fulk Sandells and John Richardson, who were friends of Anne's late father. They put up a bond—a large amount of money—guaranteeing that the wedding would take place. The two men also requested that only a single reading of the banns take place. Banns are public readings in church of a couple's intention to get married. These readings are intended to allow other members of the parish to voice any objections to the wedding. Under normal circumstances, a clergyman would read the banns on three consecutive Sundays. However, there were periods during the annual church calendar when weddings could not take place. By late November, one of these periods, Christmastime, was fast approaching. Someone wanted to make sure the marriage took place—and took place right away.

There was a reason for all this haste. Anne was already two to three months pregnant. If the marriage didn't happen right away, it wouldn't have taken place for several more weeks because of the ban on weddings during the Christmas season.

Anne was a fairly close neighbor of the Shakespeares. She lived in the village of Shottery, which was only a mile or two from Stratford. Anne's father had died, and she lived with her stepmother and three stepbrothers. It couldn't have been a comfortable arrangement. On the other hand, with her father dead, Anne was "her own woman." She was free to make her own decisions. However, Anne was past the usual age of marriage for an Elizabethan woman. She would have been competing against women considerably younger than she was for a relative handful of men to take as a husband. Perhaps she saw William as her last hope for marriage. Some scholars speculate that she may have wanted the teenager to get her pregnant and encouraged secret meetings between the two of them.

We don't know what John and Mary Shakespeare thought of the wedding. Under the terms of her father's will, Anne's dowry was not very large. John Shakespeare may have hoped for a larger dowry to help with his financial problems. Yet he had known Anne's father. Perhaps he felt obligated to persuade his son to "do the right thing."

Shakespeare may well have needed some persuading. Historically, relatively few eighteen-year-old males have been particularly eager to get married. A few commentators suggest an even more curious scenario. They maintain that the marriage licenses were actually granted to William to marry two different women. Anna Whateley may have been much closer to Shakespeare's age. She may have been the woman he really wanted to marry. These commentators say that Shakespeare panicked when he learned Anne Hathaway was pregnant. He quickly obtained a license to marry Anna Whateley, but he wasn't quick enough. The two wealthy farmers were hot on his tracks. They dragged him back to Stratford to marry Anne Hathaway.

Most scholars dismiss this idea. They believe that the clerk, who was probably overworked, simply made a mistake one day and corrected it the next. Whatever the explanation, there is no doubt that Anne Hathaway was the woman who became Mrs. William Shakespeare.

The couple almost certainly settled into the home of Shakespeare's parents. Their daughter, Susanna, was born on May 26 the following year. At the end of January 1585, Anne gave birth to twins, a boy and a girl. They were named Judith and Hamnet, after two friends of Shakespeare's, Judith and Hamnet Sadler. (Thirteen years later, the Sadlers returned the favor. They named their son William.)

Shakespeare now had three children of his own. Because he was still living at home, there would have been at least three other children, too. His youngest brother, Edmund, was only two years older than Susanna.

We don't have any direct clues about his state of mind during this time. We don't even know what he was doing for a living. His father probably insisted that he pay for his family's keep. He could have helped his father directly or found some other type of work.

The plays William would later write may shed some light on his feelings. For example, Romeo, even younger than Shakespeare at that time, says: ". . . this I pray, that thou marryest us today." (*Romeo and Juliet,* II. iii. 63–64) But Romeo is exceptional in being a very young man who wants to get married right away. In one of Shakespeare's earliest plays, a character says:

For what is wedlock forced but a hell,
An age of discord and continual strife,
Whereas the contrary bringeth bliss,
And is a pattern of celestial peace. (*Henry VI,* Part 1, V. v. 62–65)

Shakespeare never forgot this theme of not rushing into marriage. In one of his very last plays, *The Tempest,* he directly addresses the subject of forced marriage: ". . . disdain, and discord shall bestrew / The union of your bed . . . You will hate it both," he wrote. (IV. i. 20–22) He may well have been speaking from personal experience.

He may have also felt that he married too young. "A young man married is a man that's marred," he wrote in *All's Well That Ends Well.* (II. iii. 293)

33

He expressed a somewhat related idea in another play:

Let still the woman take
An elder than herself; so wears she to him,
So sways she level in her husband's heart;
For, boy, however we do praise ourselves,
Our fancies are more giddy and unfirm,
More longing, wavering, sooner lost and worn,
Than women's are. (*Twelfth Night*, II. iv. 29–35)

In other words, teenage boys are more flighty than girls of the same age. It is easier for girls, with their greater maturity, to adjust to their husbands.

No one will ever know his feelings about his wife with any degree of certainty, but the man who wrote some of the greatest lines of love poetry of all time seems never to have used his gift with his wife. There are no surviving love letters—if there ever were any. Even more frustrating to historians, nothing is known about Anne herself. Scholars speculate that she was illiterate—the common situation of most

In this poster of Shakespeare's famous tragedy *Othello*, the protagonist, Othello, clutches a dagger as he jealously peers down at his sleeping wife, Desdemona. In the play, rather than stabbing her to death, he smothers her with a pillow.

women at that time. If she was, it could explain why Shakespeare never wrote love letters. She couldn't have read them.

We know absolutely nothing of Shakespeare's feelings toward his wife. The only clues are the many passages in his plays. Shakespeare scholar Dennis Kay observes, "There is enough material to feed the suspicion that Shakespeare felt trapped, that his youthful folly with a woman already moving rapidly out of the marriageable range was something for which he was conscious of having to pay, and pay dearly."[1]

There may be another clue to his feelings. Nearly all of his comedies end with marriages. Perhaps he wanted us to believe that the new couples would live "happily ever after," yet his plays rarely depict a happy marriage and family life. Even the "happy couples" can't maintain that spirit for very long. One of his most famous characters, Othello, passionately loves his new bride, Desdemona. She continually tells him that she feels the same way, yet it takes very little to convince Othello that Desdemona has been unfaithful to him. In the end, he murders her.

Perhaps Shakespeare's most famous study of a married couple is *Macbeth*. We don't know how much genuine love Macbeth and Lady Macbeth feel for each other. What we do know is that she is very ambitious for him. This ambition leads to murder and open warfare. It also drives them apart.

Sometimes marriage in Shakespeare's plays descends into insults and outright hostility. In *King Lear*, the Duke of Albany tells his wife, Goneril, "You are not worth the dust which the rude wind / Blows in your face." (IV. ii. 30–31)

These and many similar passages would all come in the future. When the twins were born—their baptism is recorded in the same ledger as his own—Shakespeare was twenty-one. For many people, that is the age when the curtain begins to rise on their lives. At this time for Shakespeare, the curtain on his life's story came crashing down.

The Development of Drama in England

Drama in England most likely began in churches. The festivals surrounding Christmas and Easter probably involved primitive dramas. The priest would read a few lines from the Bible, then all or part of the congregation would respond.

Over time, the responses became longer and more dramatic, sometimes even with some elementary scenery. By the twelfth century, liturgical drama had emerged. These relatively lengthy productions dramatized parts of the life of Christ. They were presented inside the church, at first in Latin, then often in English. The plays became increasingly complicated. Finally they grew so large that they had to be moved outside. The subject matter changed as well. Other parts of the Bible came to be presented. Many scenes were staged on carts that would travel around town. Sound effects were introduced.

Eventually guilds—groups of different tradesmen and craftsmen—took over as the primary sponsors. The plays began to separate from the actual church liturgy. They became one of two types: miracle plays and mystery plays (*mystery* comes from a Latin word meaning "handcraft," which was the specialty of the guilds).

Miracle plays were based on the Virgin Mary or the lives of the saints, while mystery plays were taken from the Bible. Many were presented in elaborate cycles of up to forty-eight relatively short plays. These cycles dealt with a single theme, such as the Christian history of the world—from the Creation to the Last Judgment, when the world is destroyed and nonbelievers face eternal damnation. The plays began to incorporate other elements, such as wandering minstrels and adaptations for secular festivals. While the subject matter was still religious, entertainment value was becoming more and more important.

The next development was the morality play, which flourished in the fourteenth century. These plays moved away from direct references to the Bible and showed different moral values at work. Typically a character would be subjected to temptation by one or more sins. The play would show the character's struggle and how he emerged triumphant in the end.

The morality plays also apparently marked the beginning of traveling troupes of players, or actors. They would travel from town to town, often performing in the courtyards of inns. In an era where there was almost no public entertainment, their visits usually attracted large crowds.

Morality plays were soon followed by interludes. These were very short plays, sometimes performed during banquets to provide distraction as one course was cleared away and another was presented. While interludes still dealt with moral issues, they were more realistic in their presentations. Entertainment was becoming even more important.

In the middle of the sixteenth century, the Renaissance was well under way in England. The works of classical writers became widely available, including comic and tragic plays. One of the most influential writers was the ancient Roman dramatist Seneca. He wrote tragedies in which horror

Miracle plays often featured Mary and Jesus.

was a common element. In 1561, *Gorboduc* was the first English play to follow the model of Seneca. By then, at least two successful comedies—*Ralph Roister Doister and Gammer Gurton's Needle*—had already been produced.

These new works shared several common elements. They used classical plots but were set in the English landscape. There was virtually no trace of religion. And they were still being performed by traveling companies. More and more of these troupes were under the protection of a nobleman, because increasingly strict regulations were being placed on the activities of wandering actors.

The next step, while logical, represented a radical development. In 1576, James Burbage built the first permanent arena to present plays. He called it The Theatre, after a Greek word which means "to look at." Perhaps he thought that a "classical" name might make his enterprise more legitimate. Actors had a dubious reputation. He deliberately built The Theatre just outside London so that his business wouldn't be as tightly regulated.

His theater included a solid stage—an important innovation. The stages in inn yards were mounted on trestles, so they weren't very sturdy. A secure stage greatly increased the range of what actors could do.

The stage was set for the Golden Age of the English theater.

GREENES,

GROATS-VVORTH

of witte, bought with a
million of Repentance.

Deſcribing the follie of youth, the falſhood of maks-
ſhifte flatterers, the miſerie of the negligent,
and miſchiefes of deceiuing
Courtezans.

Written before his death and publiſhed at his
dyeing requeſt.

Fælicem fuiſſe infauſtum.

LONDON
Imprinted for William Wright.
1 5 9 2.

The title page of *Groatsworth of Wit,* written by a playwright named Robert Greene. Its publication in 1592 provides some of the earliest evidence for Shakespeare's newfound success as a playwright.

Chapter 4

The Lost Years

In 1592, a dying playwright in London named Robert Greene used some of his little remaining energy to write a savage attack on a rising new competitor. Greene was a very bitter man. He was only four years older than Shakespeare, yet he was about to die. His wife had abandoned him, as had his fellow actors. They left town without a second thought when he was too ill to travel with them.

Greene's attack was called *Greene's Groatsworth of Wit, Bought with a Million of Repentance. Describing the Folly of Youth, the Falsehood of Makeshift Flatterers, the Misery of the Negligent, and Mischiefs of Deceiving Courtesans.* He especially warned his colleagues to beware of

An upstart crow, beautified with our feathers, that with his
Tiger's heart wrapped in a player's hide supposes he is as well able to
bombast out a blank verse as the best of you: and being an absolute
Johannes factotum, is in his own conceit the only Shake-scene in a country.[1]

Scholars have no doubt that the "upstart crow," sarcastically referred to as "Shake-scene," is William Shakespeare. Greene's use of "*Johannes factotum*" is a slam at Shakespeare's supposed lack of learning. A *Johannes factotum* is a sort of a jack-of-all-trades, a man whose knowledge comes from practical experience rather than a university education. It was a sore spot with Greene that a man with street smarts was more popular than he.

Greene's vitriol is important because it provides the first firm evidence about Shakespeare's life since the birth of his twins was registered early in 1585. At that time, he was still in Stratford. There was nothing to indicate that he had any special interest in the theater. When Greene published *Groatsworth*, Shakespeare was an established playwright in London and a threat to Greene's livelihood. It would have been pointless to attack someone who wasn't well known.

This seven-year gap—generally termed "the lost years"—is especially frustrating. There is no way of knowing what happened during this important period in Shakespeare's life. In particular, scholars would like to know what inspired him to write. And when did he decide to try to make his fortune in the theater?

The least likely scenario is that Shakespeare remained in Stratford during most of this period, helping his father, providing for his wife and children, and somehow finding the time to write plays on the side. He wouldn't have seen much opportunity for advancement in Stratford. Like his father, he was undoubtedly ambitious for a better life. At some point he must have concluded that the theater provided his best route for that better life.

Yet with three small children and the responsibility to support them, the theater would have been only a distant dream. He simply would have been too busy to become an actor and to learn how to write plays. It seems almost certain, then, that he left Stratford. Living there would have been too constraining for his ambition.

He must have left town—and left his family behind—while the twins were still toddlers. We know nothing of any discussions that he had with his wife or his parents about this radical move, but in one respect the decision may have been easy. Going away would have been much easier with Anne and the children living with his parents. He knew his parents would take care of them.

Some possibilities have been suggested for why he left Stratford. His plays bristle with legal references, some of them very detailed. These references could have come from firsthand experience working for a lawyer. He may have taught school. However, there is no record that he earned the license a schoolteacher would have needed. Most teachers had a university education, something Shakespeare never had.

It is also possible that he may have gotten into some legal trouble. There is a story that he was caught poaching deer on the lands of a local nobleman and punished. There may have been a threat of further retribution if he stayed around.

Anne Hathaway's Cottage, where Anne lived before she married Shakespeare. Now a popular tourist attraction, it is located about a mile from Stratford in the village of Shottery. It is large for its era, containing a dozen rooms.

A few people even speculate that Shakespeare was out of the country, and that he may have become a soldier. He did write realistic battle scenes in many of his plays.

What seems most likely is that the continual visits of acting companies to Stratford—in some years, as many as five or six different troupes would perform—convinced the young man that the theater was where he wanted to make his living. There is nothing unusual about that. Many young people grow up today wanting to become actors.

In an interesting coincidence, a troupe of players known as the Queen's Men performed at Stratford in 1587. Sponsored by Queen Elizabeth, they were the best-known group of actors at the time. Just before their arrival in Stratford, one actor in the troupe killed another in a drunken fight. Suddenly the Queen's Men were short one actor. Did they hire William Shakespeare—probably no stranger to the stage, although somewhat inexperienced—to replace the dead man? Did he take that opportunity to join the company and escape from Stratford?

In one of Shakespeare's final plays, a character says, "I would there were no age between ten and three-and-twenty [twenty-three], or that youth would sleep out the rest; for there is nothing in the between but getting wenches with child, wronging the ancientry, stealing, fighting." (*The Winter's Tale*, III. iii. 59–63) Putting twenty-three at the upper end of this scale may well be significant—for that was precisely his age when the short-handed Queen's Men came to town. If he joined them at this time, it would have marked one of the remarkable strokes of luck that seem to have distinguished his career and helped to make it possible.

Another stroke was the fact that acting had become more regulated and more commercialized. For decades, if not centuries, troupes of traveling players had performed on improvised stages. These included the large halls of noblemen. The courtyards of inns were another common venue.

The English Parliament had been concerned that groups of "roving vagabonds" were claiming to be actors. In many cases, these groups were little more than criminals. They claimed to be actors to serve as a cover for their illegal activities. In 1572, Parliament cracked down. "Players" would have to be sponsored by a nobleman. If not, punishment was harsh. For the first violation, offenders would be whipped and have a hot poker pushed into their earlobes. For the second, they had to work in virtual slavery in a household for two years. The third conviction carried the death penalty.

As the one-time wandering troupes became more formalized and more organized, they were increasingly concerned with their profits. Traveling around the countryside could be a hit-and-miss proposition. The size of the paying audience was uncertain. Being constantly on the road created another strain. Consequently, more and more companies began performing in London. There they could be more confident of attracting large audiences. It was easier to find backstage personnel. They could settle down and live for extended periods in familiar surroundings. While many continued to tour, their periods of residency in London were the primary source of income.

The logical development of this increasing emphasis on London came in 1576, when James Burbage built a structure intended specifically to present plays. It was an historic event. Burbage may have recognized the significance of what he was doing. He called his new building The Theatre, the same word the Greeks had used more than two thousand years earlier for the sites of their plays.

Burbage's theater was very different from its predecessors. Greek theaters were built into the sides of hills, which created a natural bowl for spectator seating. Burbage didn't have a hill. He built an enlarged version of the courtyards in which plays had been performed for centuries. The Theatre became an immediate success. Soon a rival theater was erected close by. Others would follow.

They all followed the same basic model as The Theatre, which was circular. The stage was covered and thrust partway into the "courtyard." Many spectators were at eye level with the elevated stage, in an area that somewhat resembled a modern-day mosh pit. Admission to this area was the least expensive, but people there had to stand during the entire performance. They had no protection against rain. Many arrived drunk and stayed that way. These "groundlings" had to be entertained or they'd become restless. Playwrights soon learned to insert jokes—many that we would today consider as dirty—to keep them entertained. If they didn't, the groundlings would shout insults at the actors. Some would even throw rotten fruit and other missiles onto the stage.

Covered balconies extended around the theater from one side of the stage to the other. People who sat there paid more for the performance. They didn't mind. They didn't want to be around the groundlings. For one reason, sitting in the balcony showed that one was literally of a higher status than the groundlings. Another reason had to do with personal hygiene. Many people were infested with fleas. It was common for well-to-do people, especially women, to carry small dogs with them. The animals served a practical function. Fleas would hop off their human hosts and begin dining off the little dogs instead of their owners. It was much more comfortable to sit and allow the pet to rest on one's lap than to stand and hold the animal.

There was no mass media to provide notice of upcoming performances. Theaters hoisted a flag on a tall pole to announce a performance that day. Word of mouth was also important. News of a hit play quickly circulated throughout the city. Plays were always performed in daylight. It would be too dangerous and too expensive to provide enough lanterns and candles to provide illumination at night.

The stage was relatively small, and there wasn't much scenery. Sometimes a boy would walk onto the stage carrying a sign that established the location, or an actor would have a line early in a scene that indicated where he was.

Actors at that time were all males. Women were not permitted on stage. Boys played most women's parts. Their high-pitched voices would resemble those of women. Sometimes an adult would take on a female role, especially if the character was supposed to be funny or had a low-pitched voice.

There were some primitive special effects. Smoke could be released to cover an actor's entrance or exit. Rolling a cannonball around on the floor of the upper level mimicked the sound of thunder. Some actors would be lowered onto the stage. Because the stage was elevated several feet above the ground, a trapdoor could be used if an actor needed to drop out of sight. Actors often used pig's blood to make their death scenes more realistic.

Not everyone liked the new theaters. Their main enemies were the Puritans, who thought that going to plays encouraged immoral behavior. They also thought that the theaters attracted bad elements. There was some truth to those charges. Cut-purses, the Elizabethan equivalent of today's pickpockets, would take advantage of the fact that nearly everyone—men and women alike—carried money in purses tied to their belts with string. The thieves would wait until the person carrying the purse was distracted, then they would quickly slice the strings with sharp knives and flee with what they had stolen. There were even "schools" that taught boys their "trade." Theaters provided ideal locations to put their lessons to good effect.

A third stroke of good fortune in Shakespeare's career can definitely be dated. Wherever Shakespeare was in 1588, the young man undoubtedly joined with his countrymen in celebrating the defeat of the Spanish Armada. The victory was the culmination of the long-simmering hostility between England and Spain that began when Henry VIII tried to divorce Catherine. The primary purpose of the Armada was to remove Queen Elizabeth from the throne and replace her with a Catholic monarch. If this had happened, England would have once again become a Catholic country. The conditions in which Shakespeare was allowed to flourish would not have existed.

Still another factor was the rise of the so-called "university wits" toward the end of the 1580s. These were university-educated men who had turned to writing plays. Their extensive knowledge of classical literature helped complete the transformation of plays from religious to secular subjects. Soon the wits dominated the stage. They developed a technique that Shakespeare would later perfect.

This technique was called blank verse. Nearly every line in their plays was written in iambic pentameter (pronounced eye-AM-bik pen-TAA-muh-tur). An iamb (EYE-am) is a poetic foot consisting of an unaccented syllable followed by an accented syllable. *Pentameter* means that there are five feet to each line. For example, one of Shakespeare's most famous lines is "A horse! A horse! My kingdom for a horse!" (*Richard III*, V. iv. 7). An actor would say the line: "a HORSE! a HORSE! my KING-dom

FOR a HORSE!" The syllables in lowercase letters are not emphasized, while the ones in capital letters are.

In blank verse, the lines rarely rhyme with each other. Occasionally the final two lines do rhyme, in which case they are called a couplet.

The university wits included John Lyly, Thomas Nashe, George Peele, Thomas Watson, Thomas Lodge, and even *Groatsworth* writer Robert Greene. The most famous was Christopher Marlowe, an exact contemporary of Shakespeare. His best-known line refers to Helen of Troy and the origin of the Trojan War: "Is this the face that launched a thousand ships?" (*The Tragicall History of Doctor Faustus*, V. i.) His biggest box-office success, *Tamburlaine the Great*, may have coincided with Shakespeare's arrival on the theater scene. The hero of this play is a shepherd who is utterly ruthless in his pursuit of power. He rises to rule a great empire. At the end, he boasts about all the people he has killed. *Tamburlaine* was completely different from the morality plays and mystery plays that had preceded it.

In short, the times were ideal for the emergence of William Shakespeare. Of course, he had no way of knowing that. All he knew was that he had chosen a difficult path. Despite the popularity of plays, the people who wrote and performed them weren't assured of making a lot of money. They were often criticized for being immoral. They didn't enjoy much social status.

Nevertheless, as author Park Honan observes, "On a day of doubtful promise to himself, [Shakespeare] would have had to bid farewell to his parents, three small children, and Anne, and set out on a road leading to the teeming, colourful, and oddly dangerous south."[2]

No one could have possibly known that waiting at the end of the road was the reputation of "the finest author of all time."

The Spanish Armada

In Shakespeare's time, relations between Spain and England had been complicated for many years. Henry's efforts to obtain a divorce from his Spanish-born Queen Catherine were just the beginning.

The religious turmoil that followed when his daughters Mary and then Elizabeth assumed the throne served to worsen the relationship. In 1570, Pope Pius V excommunicated Elizabeth and said that any Catholic who fought against her would be forgiven of his sins. Three years later King Philip II of Spain signed a treaty with the Pope. It called for an invasion of England and replacing Elizabeth with a suitable Catholic.

Religion wasn't the only factor. English sea captains, notably Sir Francis Drake, raided Spanish galleons that carried treasure from the New World back to Spain. England was also aiding Protestants in the Netherlands in their effort to throw off Spanish rule.

The Duke of Parma, the Spanish commander in the Netherlands, had an army of more than 20,000 men that could also be used to invade England. Cumbersome, slow-moving barges were the only way of getting all those soldiers across the English Channel. They would be easy prey for English warships. The solution was providing an overwhelming Spanish fleet, or armada, of warships and transports to protect them.

In 1584 Philip began building his armada. The ambitious project took several years. Once completed, it was under the command of the Duke of Medina Sidonia, a good administrator who didn't know much about ships. He set sail from Lisbon, Portugal, on May 28, 1588. Due to storms and other delays, the opposing fleets didn't meet for nearly two months. When they did, they sailed along the southern coast of England in an easterly direction for about a week. They had three brief battles. Little damage was done to either side.

Even though they were outnumbered, the English had several advantages. They were fighting in familiar home waters. Their ships were faster and easier to maneuver, which enabled them to stay between the Spanish fleet and the land. The English cannons were also capable of firing farther, so they could shoot at the Spanish and remain out of range of return fire. The Spanish strategy was to get alongside the enemy so that they could board. They had many more men and could have overrun the English ships, but they could never get close enough.

The Spanish crossed the English Channel and anchored off Calais, France. They were supposed to meet the troops led by the Duke of Parma. Because of a communication failure, the duke's troops weren't there. The English deliberately set several of their

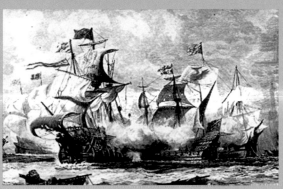

The English fleet attacks the Spanish Armada.

own ships on fire. With no one aboard, they slowly drifted toward the Spanish fleet. At the sight of these fire ships, the Spanish crews panicked. They cut their anchor cables and fled to the north.

The English pursued them. The two sides met off the French town of Gravelines. The English sank or damaged about a dozen Spanish ships, but they ran out of ammunition. The Spanish didn't know that. The English ships bluffed them. They acted as if they were going to attack again. The Spanish captains were frightened. Pursued by the English, they fled northward from the scene of the battle. Because of the direction of the wind, the Spanish ships couldn't turn around. Finally the Duke of Medina Sidonia, still in overall command, decided to keep going. The Armada sailed past the northern end of Scotland and Ireland out into the open sea. Then the ships swung south and headed home.

Nature defeated this plan. Severe storms arose, and dozens of Spanish ships sank in the open sea or were driven aground. Some crews drowned. Others made their way to shore. Most were killed by the people who found them. A few were sheltered by sympathetic Irish Catholics.

The battered survivors finally made their way back to Spain. The original fleet had lost between one-third and one-half of its ships. The English believed that their victory had been a sign of divine intervention. Relations between the two countries remained strained.

In 1587, Pope Sixtus V had promised a large sum of money to help pay for the invasion. When he saw the result, he refused to pay a cent. Philip was unhappy with the decision and protested. Sixtus's death in 1590 ended the dispute.

Shakespeare arrived in London around 1587. He took advantage of some fortunate turns of events and his own natural talent to become an accomplished playwright.

Chapter
5

Into (and out of?) London

Shakespeare's journey to London wouldn't have taken very long if he had gone there directly. In those days, people were accustomed to covering long distances on foot. He could easily have walked the one hundred miles in three or four days.

According to one story, that is exactly what happened. Arriving in London with almost no money, he quickly obtained a job at a theater as a "waiter." Many people who attended plays arrived on horseback. One of their servants held their horses while their master was inside. Riders who didn't have servants needed a waiter—the equivalent of today's parking valet. Apparently Shakespeare had a good reputation in this position: "In this office he became so conspicuous for his care and readiness that in a short time every man as he alighted called for *Will. Shakespeare* and scarcely any other waiter was trusted with a horse while *Will. Shakespeare* could be had," wrote Samuel Johnson, a famous English writer who lived in the eighteenth century. "This was the first dawn of better fortune."[1]

As with so many other stories about Shakespeare, there is no way of knowing whether it is true or not. It's just as likely that he was with the Queen's Men, happily serving as a replacement for the man who had been murdered a few days earlier. In that case, the journey to London probably would have taken several weeks. The company would have performed in different towns before returning to the city. For the young would-be actor and playwright, each day was a fresh delight. He was taking a crash-course in theatrical production and management.

According to his first biographer, Nicholas Rowe, these two versions actually came together at Burbage's Theatre, the home of the Queen's Men. Regardless of how he got there, Shakespeare's "first office in the theatre was that of prompter's attendant, whose employment it is to give the performers notice to be ready to enter, as often as the business of the play requires their appearance on the stage."[2] It was humble work, but Shakespeare had his foot in the door. From there, it would have been a natural progression to bit parts. Writing would have been another natural progression. The young man would have wanted to make himself as useful as possible, and at some point—probably relatively early in his career—Shakespeare must have realized that he was better at writing than acting.

For a young man who had spent his entire life in the country, the first few days and weeks in London must have been a feast for the senses. It was one of the largest cities in Europe, with a population that likely exceeded 200,000.There was so much to see: large buildings, seemingly endless streets, so many different types of people, even ships from foreign countries tied up at docks along the Thames River.

Another sight was London Bridge, which spanned the Thames River to connect the city to the southern part of the country. It was massive, with twenty separate sections. It was also the scene of frequent traffic jams. The crowding was intensified because many merchants had built houses on the bridge. The lowest floor of the homes displayed their wares, with the upper floors for living.

It's likely that smell provided Shakespeare's first sensory experiences of the city. According to some reports, people typically began smelling London while they were still more than twenty miles away. The odors came from many sources. Human and animal waste, wood smoke, and rotten food were only a few.

The smells also extended to the personal level, especially among common people. People rarely bathed or changed clothes. Oral hygiene was almost nonexistent. Shakespeare's play *Julius Caesar* has a scene that Shakespeare must have drawn from his own experience. A Roman nobleman sarcastically explains the crowd's behavior to a friend after Caesar has just turned down an opportunity to be crowned as the King of Rome:

> the rabblement hooted and clapped their
> chapped hands and threw up their sweaty night-caps
> and uttered such a deal of stinking breath because
> Caesar refused the crown that it had almost choked

Caesar; for he swounded and fell down at it: and

for mine own part, I durst not laugh, for fear of

opening my lips and receiving the bad air. (I. ii. 251–257)

A good portion of the city's energy came from shoppers. In an era before refrigeration, many people made daily purchases of fish, meat, milk, and other foods that spoiled quickly. More than a dozen markets—most of them dealing with a narrow range of commodities—attracted thousands of people every day. What is likely the world's first shopping mall—the Royal Exchange—was well established by the time Shakespeare arrived.

Foreign visitors were surprised at the number of women who were in the streets on a regular basis. One from Venice noted: "The Englishwomen have great freedom to go out of the home without menfolk; the husbands do not spend their time in household jobs but the women themselves carry the goods if they are poor . . . or make their maids do so if they have them."[3]

There was a great deal of violence. Gangs of young men freely wandered through the city, thinking nothing of beating up or even killing anyone they felt like. Thievery was

The London Bridge Shakespeare knew was torn down in 1831. The "new" London Bridge (above) replaced it. In Shakespeare's time, the bridge was lined with shops.

very common. Prostitution ran rampant. According to contemporary reports, prostitutes would sometimes go into churches to find their customers.

It was a young city. "It has been estimated that half of the urban population was under the age of twenty years," notes Ackroyd. "This is what rendered it so strident, so tough, so excitable. . . . Londoners were often compared to a swarm of bees, quick to congregate and to act in instinctive union."[4]

Ackroyd adds another factor. Average life expectancy was not very high. As a result, he continues, Londoners "were consigned to a short burst of existence with the evidence of disease and mortality all around them. Their experience was all the more vital and intense. This was the proper context for the growth of drama."[5]

In short, William Shakespeare's decision to seek his fortune in London couldn't have come at a better time. Once the initial surge of excitement at being in London had subsided, he began working in earnest. There were enormous demands on theatrical companies. Survival depended on getting many of the same paying customers back on a regular basis. The majority didn't want to see the same play over and over again. Each company therefore needed a number of new plays every year. There would have been plenty of work for someone with writing talent. William Shakespeare had that kind of talent.

There are a few indications that Shakespeare didn't have much of a learning curve as a playwright, especially if he didn't leave Stratford until 1587. It is possible that he had completed his first play by the end of that year—no one knows for certain. Scholars agree on a rough order in which Shakespeare's plays were written, but in many cases, especially at the beginning, it is difficult to pin them down to exact dates.

One candidate for Shakespeare's first play is *Two Gentlemen of Verona*. Like nearly all of his plays, it has an important comic character. This character, Launce, has a dog that joins him on stage. Today we are accustomed to seeing animals in films or plays. These animals don't just come in off the street. They are highly trained "professionals." This would have been just as true in Shakespeare's era. Playwrights couldn't use any old mutt.

The Queen's Men had a famous comic actor named Richard Tarlton. He is the only actor on record at that time with a trained dog. Tarlton died in 1588. This timing suggests that *Two Gentlemen of Verona* may have been written by then, but it is hardly conclusive proof. Shakespeare might have written the part with some other actor in mind. It is also possible that there was another actor with a trained dog who simply didn't leave behind a record.

Another candidate is *Titus Andronicus*, Shakespeare's first tragedy. It is filled with revenge and gory murders. It begins with two brothers murdering a man. They assault the man's wife—on her husband's corpse. They cut out her tongue and amputate her hands so that she can't testify against them. When help arrives, she uses what's left of her arms to hold a stick and scratch out their names in the dirt. Her father finds the two brothers and kills them. He puts their bones into a flour mill, grinds them up, and uses the flour to make a pie. He serves the pie to their mother. Only two of the play's leading characters are still alive at the end. One buries the other waist-deep in the earth. He will die by starvation.

A third possibility for his first play is *The Taming of the Shrew*, which is much better known today than the other two. Several men want to marry a young woman named Bianca, but her father won't allow the girl to wed until her older sister, Katherine, has been married. Men fear Katherine. She is not "ladylike." No man thinks that he can "tame" her. Then Petruchio, the hero, comes along. He takes a bet that he is the man to tame her. He marries her almost forcibly and treats her miserably. Bianca's marriage follows soon afterward. At a banquet at the end of the play, Petruchio and Bianca's husband bet which wife will be more obedient.

Bianca shows some spirit when her husband sends word for her to appear right away. She refuses. When Petruchio summons Katherine, she responds immediately. Pulling the stubborn Bianca along with her, she says, "Thy husband is thy lord, thy life, thy keeper. . . . Such duty as the subject owes the prince / Even such a woman oweth to her husband . . . And place your hands below your husband's foot." (V. ii. 146, 155–156, 179).

Today, those words may sound dreadful, but words on a page aren't the same as words on a stage. Many actresses give this speech an ironic twist. Perhaps Katherine knows about the bet and wants to help Petruchio win it. It would mean more money for their household, after all. That scheme would appeal to Shakespeare's business sense. As events would soon reveal, he was an excellent businessman. It was a talent he had learned from his father.

Yet another possibility for Shakespeare's first play arises from contemporary culture. With the defeat of the Spanish Armada still fresh in everyone's mind, England was feeling a surge of national pride. English citizens became especially interested in their recent history. Elizabeth's rocky rise to rule was the culmination of more than two centuries of turbulent events. Several earlier monarchs had been overthrown as England experienced the horrors of civil war.

Shakespeare took advantage of this situation to begin writing what are known as his history plays. While these plays are based on historical facts, Shakespeare often took great liberties with the actual occurrences.

The original title of the first one was *The First Part of the Contention of the Two Famous Houses of York and Lancaster with the Death of the Good Duke Humphrey*. The second was *The True Tragedy of Richard, Duke of York, and Good King Henry the Sixth*. They are more commonly known as *Henry VI, Part Two* and *Henry VI, Part Three*. Soon he would return to many of the same characters and write the prequel, *King Henry VI, Part One*. Contemporary evidence shows that all three plays did very well at the box office.

Even though the three plays are not highly regarded today, they were radical at the time. They covered more than fifty years of history—for Elizabethans, it was recent history, not long-ago stories set in classical times. Even more startling, Shakespeare let his characters talk about their feelings and explain their reasons for doing what they did.

The plays are also notable for their realistic portrayal of King Henry VI. He had become king when he was still a baby after the death of his heroic father, Henry V. He never enjoyed a fraction of the respect that his father had commanded, even when he reached adulthood. On two occasions in *Part Three,* he tries to speak and isn't allowed to. This would have been shocking for a generation that still clung to at least a partial belief that kings were divinely inspired.

The Henry VI plays also gave rise to Shakespeare's first great villain, Richard III, which became the title of another early play. Even as Henry VI is lowered into the grave, Richard—then the Duke of Gloucester—is plotting his own rise to the throne. These plans involve treachery and murder—including killing his two nephews, who precede him in the line of succession. The play later gave rise to a famous (though unproven) story. In 1601, actor Richard Burbage was playing Richard III. Shakespeare overheard him make a date with a female fan, who invited Burbage to her house when the play was over. During the performance, Shakespeare snuck out of the theater. He went to the woman's house while Burbage was still on stage. Later that evening, Burbage arrived at the woman's house. He knocked on the door and said that "Richard III" was there. Shakespeare, who was still inside, shouted that William the Conqueror had arrived before Richard III. That was a double pun. William the Conqueror crossed over to England from France in 1066, several centuries before Richard's birth. Shakespeare was also referring to himself as William, the conqueror of women.

Just as Shakespeare's writing career began, a cloud covered it. Plagues were relatively common in that era. The plague offered an excuse for the ever-vigilant Puritans to attack the theater. One Puritan clergyman explained, "The cause of plague is sin . . . and the cause of sin are plays; therefore the cause of plague are plays."[6] Civic officials believed the plague thrived in large crowds of people. Few activities attracted larger crowds than plays. As a result, the government ordered all the theaters in London to shut down in the winter of 1592–1593. They would remain closed for nearly two years.

Many theater people wanted to continue making a living by performing. They organized temporary companies and hit the road, where conditions were believed to be much safer. Almost certainly Shakespeare stayed in London. It was risky to remain there, but he knew he had survived one bout of the plague already as a youngster. He may have felt immune. Not only that, a household of noisy small children back home in Stratford wouldn't have had much appeal.

His initial success may have puffed up his ego. Years earlier, his father had wanted to be a "gentleman." It's likely that his son took on the same ambition. The ability to write poetry was one mark of an educated gentleman. In addition, poetry was a far more respected form of writing than playwriting. With the pressure to write plays temporarily removed, the enforced idleness may have allowed him to try his hand at writing poetry.

There is a problem with this scenario. Shakespeare would have needed money on which to live. Fortunately, there was a solution close at hand. He netted a patron.

A patron was someone from the upper class or nobility with plenty of money and an affection (either real or artificial) for the arts. For the two people involved, it was usually a win-win situation. The writer's money worries would be gone. In many cases, the patron also supplied a very elegant roof over his head. In turn, the patron expected the writer to dedicate his upcoming works to him. This dedication would involve a somewhat lengthy introduction of the patron, filled with flattery. The patron would become even more impressive in the eyes of his friends.

Shakespeare's patron was the Earl of Southampton. The earl was just nineteen years old. He probably had attended some of the plays that Shakespeare had written. He was also distantly related to the playwright on his mother's side.

The earl had two homes. One was just outside of London, and the other was a country home. It's likely that Shakespeare spent extensive periods of time in both locations.

He may even have served as the personal secretary to the young man. It didn't take him long to take advantage of the earl's patronage.

Shakespeare began writing the first of an eventual 154 sonnets. The sonnet, a popular form of poetry, had been developing for centuries. Most sonnets were about love. A young woman wasn't much interested in a suitor who couldn't write a sonnet about her and his love for her.

Sonnets are difficult to write. They are subject to several demanding technical rules. They must have exactly fourteen lines. Each line is written in iambic pentameter. The poem follows a rigid rhyme scheme.

Shakespeare invented his own rhyme scheme, which can be expressed as follows: a b a b c d c d e f e f g g. Each letter stands for a different rhyme. He added another refinement. The first eight lines (the octave) set up an argument; the remaining six lines (the sestet) respond to the argument. These qualities can be seen in one of his most famous sonnets. Today it is known as Sonnet Number 18.

Shall I compare thee to a summer's day? (a)
 Thou art more lovely and more temperate: (b)
Rough winds do shake the darling buds of May, (a)
 And summer's lease hath all too short a date: (b)

Sometime too hot the eye of heaven shines, (c)
 And often is his gold complexion dimm'd; (d)
And every fair from fair sometime declines, (c)
 By chance, or nature's changing course, untrimm'd; (d)

But thy eternal summer shall not fade, (e)
 Nor lose possession of that fair thou owest; (f)
Nor shall Death brag thou wander'st in his shade, (e)
 When in eternal lines to time thou growest; (f)
  So long as men can breathe, or eyes can see, (g)
  So long lives this, and this gives life to thee. (g)

The letters in parentheses show the different rhymes (today in line two we would say TEM-puh-RUT, but Shakespeare would have pronounced it TEM-puh-RAYT). The "argument" (the first eight lines) compares the person the poet loves to a summer's day.

The problem is that summer days can be too windy or too hot. Even more important, the glories of summer eventually will fade. All the lovely plants will die.

The response to these drawbacks comes in the final six lines (the sestet). The poet explains that the feelings he has for his beloved will never fade—because he has written them down. As long as people have the ability to read, they will know the depth of his love. Most Shakespearean scholars believe that the subject of this admiration is a man, not a woman. It was customary in his era for men to speak flatteringly of each other's physical beauty.

When he wrote his first sonnets, Shakespeare had no intention of having them published. In fact, what would be his entire collection of sonnets wouldn't be published until his career was almost over.

Shakespeare had a more immediate goal in mind. In 1593, his long poem called *Venus and Adonis* appeared in print. All the tedious hours learning Latin in school paid off. The poem used one of the stories in Ovid's *Metamorphoses*. Venus, the goddess of love, is attracted to a handsome young man named Adonis. He tells her he isn't interested in her. He is too young to be romantically involved. (This may be yet another example of Shakespeare confessing that he had married at too young an age.) He would rather hunt. Venus tries everything she can think of to seduce him, but nothing works. Finally Adonis goes away. The next morning he is killed by a wild boar. Venus turns his body into a purple-and-white flower called the anemone.

Shakespeare dedicated the poem to his patron. It was a huge hit. Contemporary accounts suggest that many young men tucked a copy under their pillows when they went to sleep at night. It was reprinted nine times while Shakespeare was alive. Six more printings followed after his death.

The following year's *The Rape of Lucrece* was equally successful. It came from a story set in Roman times. Again Ovid was the major source of information. A beautiful young married woman is assaulted by a king named Tarquin. She chooses to die rather than live in dishonor. Her enraged relatives seek revenge. They force Tarquin to give up his throne. Like *Venus and Adonis*, *The Rape of Lucrece* helped to keep Shakespeare's name in the public consciousness.

It may have been at about this time that he heard the news the killing of Henry Long. The news would have been especially welcome. He knew that the theaters would soon reopen. He intended to be ready.

Shop Till They Drop

Soon after Elizabeth became queen, a merchant named Thomas Gresham wanted London to establish a commercial exchange. He believed that it would bring much more money into the city. It would serve as a magnet for merchants all over England and attract attention from the European continent. After considering his proposal,

A courtyard scene in the Royal Exchange in 1809, many years after Shakespeare's time.

the city's government agreed with him. They furnished the land it would require and also donated 100,000 bricks to help with the construction.

Work began in the late spring of 1566. Some businesses may have begun operating as early as the end of 1568. Queen Elizabeth officially opened the building in 1571, after which it became known as the Royal Exchange. It was a huge structure, with space for up to 4,000 deal-making merchants on the sprawling main floor. Another 150 specialty shops lined the surrounding gallery. A tower was used for free Sunday musical concerts during the warm summer afternoons. "The musicians of the City perform marvels of sound to the great contentment of all who hear,"[7] reported a spectator in 1576.

In all likelihood, the Royal Exchange was the first shopping mall. According to some stories, the shops were hard to rent in the beginning. When the queen toured the facility for the first time, shopkeepers snatched their goods from areas that Elizabeth had just visited and ran ahead to fill up otherwise vacant stalls.

Soon the mall idea caught on. Well-to-do Londoners loved to find so many places to spend their money in such a small area. They had a wide variety of goods from which to choose. According to London historian Liza Picard, shopkeepers carried "essentials such as mousetraps and bird-cages, shoehorns and lanterns, armourers sold new and second-hand armour—always useful—and apothecaries, booksellers, goldsmiths and glass sellers catered for impulse buying."[8]

Much of the merchandise was high-end, such as expensive jewelry, delicate porcelain, and expensive fabrics. "I must have a damasked pair of spurs!"[9] said a young diplomat on the eve of departing for a foreign assignment. These were spurs with elaborate designs carefully carved into the metal. They would presumably make him appear more important.

Someone recorded a conversation between a female shopper and one of the jewel merchants. " 'Showe me the biggest pearles, the most Orientall, and the roundest that you have,' says the lady, who asks the jeweler what properties his pearls possess. 'They have many properties,' he replies, 'But that which is most profitable unto us, It is the force they have to transporte the money from your pursse into ours.' "[10]

Apparently the Royal Exchange was noisy. According to a contemporary description, the building was "vaulted and hollow, and has such an Echo, as multiplies every word that is spoken."[11]

The Royal Exchange was very successful. Soon after his accession, King James I felt confident enough to establish another one as the population of London expanded beyond the city's original boundaries. It opened in 1609 and was known as the New Exchange. It was probably the first suburban mall. While it didn't have the same prestige as the Royal Exchange, it was apparently just as popular.

Writing a few decades later (during which time it had changed very little), noted diarist Samuel Pepys frequently recorded visits to the New Exchange. "With my wife, by coach, to the New Exchange, to buy her some things; where we saw some new-fashion pettycoats of sarcenett [high-quality soft silk cloth], with a black broad lace printed round the bottom and before, very handsome, and my wife had a mind to one of them,"[12] he wrote.

Pepys also went to the New Exchange simply to see friends and exchange gossip. "On hearing of a British sea victory over a Dutch fleet, Away go I by coach to the New Exchange, and there did spread this good news a little,"[13] he noted on another occasion.

"After seeing a play, Thence to the New Exchange, to buy some things; and, among others, my wife did give me my pair of gloves" he recorded of still another visit. "Here Mrs. Smith tells us of the great murder thereabouts on Saturday last, of one Captain Bumbridge, by one Symons, both of her acquaintance."[14]

Then, just as now, people went to the mall to shop, to gossip, and to hang out with their friends.

A model of the Globe Theatre. The groundlings—the patrons with the least money—stood for the entire performance on three sides of the thrust stage. The better-off spectators paid a little more for the privilege of sitting in one of the galleries.

Chapter 6

The Globe Theatre

In 1594 the plague warning ended—and so did Shakespeare's relationship with the Earl of Southampton. He was on his own.

He quickly landed on his feet. With the theaters open again, his primary means of livelihood was renewed. He may have resented having to give up on his desire to become a famous poet. If he did, it didn't show. By then he was regarded as one of London's best playwrights—if not the best. As well as his talent, his luck was part of the reason.

Three of his major competitors were now dead. Greene died first. Marlowe was killed in a bar brawl in 1593. Thomas Kyd, whose *Spanish Tragedy* was one of the most popular plays of the era, died shortly before the theaters reopened.

Another factor was the dissolution of the Queen's Men. The troupe had struggled ever since the death of its comic actor, Richard Tarlton, in 1588. Now two new companies emerged. One was the Admiral's Men. The other was the Lord Chamberlain's Men, of which Shakespeare was a member. Their patron was Henry Carey, Lord Hunsdon. Carey served as Lord Chamberlain to the Queen. Some of the prominent actors in the troupe were Richard Burbage (the son of the man who built The Theatre), John Heminges, and comic actor Will Kempe.

For Shakespeare, joining the Lord Chamberlain's Men proved to be a lifetime move. From then on, all his energies would be devoted to the welfare of this group. Many of the men would become his closest friends.

What he wrote played to the strengths of each of the actors. For example, Richard Burbage almost always played the principal character. That's one reason why so many of Shakespeare's earlier plays have relatively young leading characters. As Burbage grew older, so did the characters he would portray.

Shakespeare did much more than write plays for the Lord Chamberlain's Men. He acted in some minor roles and probably served as a part-time director. He was also a "sharer," or part-owner, of the group, so he had a voice in its financial operations.

The order of the plays that the newly created Lord Chamberlain's Men performed when the theaters reopened isn't certain. *Love's Labour's Lost* is one possibility. In this play, Shakespeare depicts extended scenes of royal courts that living with the Earl of Southampton would have helped create. *Romeo and Juliet* also premiered about this time, as did *A Midsummer Night's Dream*, one of the most commonly produced Shakespeare plays in the modern era. The cast includes four young people—two men and two women—who keep falling in and out of love with each other. Another level features a kingdom of the fairies. A third consists of "rude mechanicals," working men who are rehearsing a play for an upcoming royal wedding. The characters on all three levels continually interact with each other in a variety of humorous situations.

The play features the character Bottom, the first great comic role that Shakespeare created. At one point, Bottom becomes a donkey. Shakespeare has a good time with puns that are based on the connection between *Bottom* and *ass,* another word for donkey.

Apparently all these plays were huge box office successes. By 1596, two years after the theaters had reopened, there was no doubt that Shakespeare had made the right decision by leaving Stratford to seek his fortune. The future must have seemed unlimited to him. He was thirty-two, in the prime of life, with a secure and comfortable income. He had enough money to purchase a house in London. It's significant that he chose not to invite his family to rejoin him. Anne and the children remained in Stratford.

His success also paved the way for his father to reapply for the coat of arms he had unsuccessfully sought twenty-seven years earlier. It's unlikely that John Shakespeare was doing much better financially. Accordingly, the money that was necessary to renew the application almost certainly came from his son. This time the coat of arms was granted.

Shakespeare probably was motivated by more than filial love. In spite of their popularity on the stage, theater people were considered somewhat disreputable in real life. Shakespeare had always been ambitious. Spending a lot of time around aristocrats and other important people would have whetted his desire to acquire a higher social status. A coat of arms showed the importance of an individual. It signified that he was a "gentleman." It also permitted him to wear clothes that reflected this higher social status.

Just as important, a coat of arms was something that could be passed along from generation to generation. If his father was now a "gentleman," so was Shakespeare. He was very proud of his new title. Twenty years later, he signed his last will and testament as "William Shakespeare, of Stratford upon Avon in the county of Warwick, gentleman."[1]

In the midst of these successes, tragedy struck.

No one knows how often Shakespeare made the trip to Stratford to visit his family after he left home, but one time is certain. It was August 11, 1596—the day his son Hamnet was buried.

The only evidence for this family tragedy is bound up in the parish records, which indicate the date on which the boy was laid to rest. We don't know what caused Hamnet's death. Shakespeare left no surviving account of the event or of his reaction.

His grief is probably reflected in his plays. At the time of Hamnet's death, Shakespeare was working on *King John*. The play contains these lines:

Grief fills the room up of my absent child,
Lies in his bed, walks up and down with me,
Puts on his pretty looks, repeats his words,
Remembers me of all his gracious parts,
Stuffs out his vacant garments with his form. (III. iv. 93–97)

With Hamnet's death, Shakespeare lost his only direct male heir. Even though he and Anne had had three children within two years, they never had any others. That may have reflected how rarely Shakespeare returned to Stratford. It may also have reflected the damage that twins did to a woman's reproductive system in that era. In any event, Anne was now forty years old. It was too late for her to bear any more children.

The year after Hamnet's death, Shakespeare purchased a home in Stratford. Up until then, it seems likely that his family had still been living with his parents. Losing Hamnet may have been enough of a shock for Shakespeare to decide that the surviving members deserved a home of their own. And not just any home. Called New Place, it was perhaps the town's finest house. Though Shakespeare himself spent very little time living there, it was a fitting property for a playwright because it had its own dramatic history. It had been built in 1490. An earlier owner, William Bott, had murdered his daughter Isabella. For complicated reasons, Bott was never charged with a crime. He eventually sold the house to the Underhill family. William Underhill sold the home to Shakespeare.

Shakespeare's ownership soon became clouded. Before the sale, Underhill had promised the land to his son Fulke, who was then a minor. Soon afterward, Fulke murdered his father by poisoning him. The son was hanged. Fulke's crime and death confused the title to the property until 1602, when the younger son, Hercules Underhill, came of age. He quickly confirmed the sale.

The memory of the murderous hatreds that can exist within families may have haunted Shakespeare's imagination. All four of his great tragedies—*Hamlet, Othello, Macbeth*, and *King Lear*—were written after the sale. All four examine the potentially lethal relationships among family members.

In 1598, he became involved in another property dispute. When James Burbage built The Theatre in 1576, he leased the land on which the structure stood. In 1597, the lease came up for renewal. The landowner drove a hard bargain—so hard, in fact, that the Lord Chamberlain's Men either could not or would not accept. The stress and strain may have been one reason why James Burbage dropped dead during the negotiations.

The uncertain situation dragged on for more than a year and a half. Late in 1598, the landlord threatened to demolish The Theatre. The troupe decided on a desperate and daring move. Assisted by a few other men, they gathered at the theater at dusk a few days after Christmas. It was one of the longest nights of the year. Working as quietly as possible, they spent the entire night dismantling the building in the bitter cold. They saved the lumber and the furnishings and hauled them across London Bridge. Almost immediately they began putting the building back together.

Not surprisingly, the property owner was furious. He took the company to court. But the company members had acted within their rights. It was true that they didn't own the land, but according to the terms of the lease, they owned every stick of wood that they had used to construct the theater.

Reassembly was complete by May 1599. What was known as the Globe Theatre triumphantly opened. As a part owner, Shakespeare was entitled to a significant share of the profits. The Globe soon established a reputation as the best-equipped theater in London. With a capacity of between 2,500 and 3,000 spectators, it almost certainly was the largest.

For the rest of his career, *the Globe Theatre* would be synonymous with *Shakespeare*. It would be the scene of many of his greatest triumphs and would help to make him even more wealthy and famous.

It would also be the scene of Kempe's departure from the company. Kempe was the troupe's best comic actor. One of his most famous parts had been Falstaff in the history plays *Henry IV, Part One* and *Part Two*, which had played a few years earlier. Queen Elizabeth liked Falstaff so much that she had asked Shakespeare to write a play in which he was the main character. Shakespeare was happy to oblige. The result was the *Merry Wives of Windsor*. It was one of his few original plots. No one realized it at the time, but it was likely Kempe's last major theatrical role. He left the company soon afterward.

As Shakespeare historian Michael Wood points out, "A stand-up comic, a virtuoso song and dance man and an unpredictable and uproarious ad libber, Kempe had been the darling of the groundlings. But Shakespeare and the rest of the company were moving toward higher-class shows with a more refined and fixed text, and it may be that 'artistic disagreements' were the cause of Kempe's departure."[2]

Robert Armin eventually replaced Kempe. He wasn't as obviously funny as Kempe had been, so Shakespeare wrote a different type of humor for him. Armin still made audiences laugh, but often he cut to the pain beneath the laughter. Many of his speeches reveal deep psychological truths. In a number of plays, he is the only person with enough courage to tell a king or other important person what he really thinks of him.

Armin, Shakespeare, and the other members of the company came uncomfortably close to an unpleasant end in 1601. By that time, Queen Elizabeth was in her late sixties. She had ruled for forty-three years. Before becoming queen, she spent much of her energy simply trying to stay alive while her brother and sister ruled the country. After ascending the throne, there were many more demands on her stamina. She knew that some of her countrymen wanted her dead. So did many foreign powers, especially Spain. The strain of governing under these conditions was catching up with her. She was exhausted.

For many years, Robert Devereaux, the Earl of Essex, had been one of Elizabeth's strongest supporters. He was one of the most popular men in England. He was also one of the most ambitious. Now Essex decided that Elizabeth was past her prime. He wanted to turn his popularity into something more. He wanted to kill the queen and rule in her place. Some of England's highest-ranking noblemen supported him. He made careful plans. Two days before the date of his planned uprising, he approached Shakespeare's troupe. He wanted them to perform Shakespeare's *Richard II*. The actors protested. The play had been written about a decade earlier. It was old news. Hardly anyone was likely to attend.

Essex pulled out his wallet and offered them a large sum of money. That was all it took. No matter how many paying customers actually showed up, the show would turn a profit. Meanwhile, Essex was actually putting the Lord Chamberlain's Men in jeopardy.

In the play, Richard is portrayed as a weak king. He is overthrown by a strong nobleman named Henry Bolingbroke. Henry becomes king and rules as Henry IV. Essex hoped that the playgoers would "get it": Elizabeth was Richard and he was Henry.

His plan flopped. The people who attended the play apparently didn't make the connection. Nor did they respond as he had hoped they would when he rose against Elizabeth. He had almost no support. He was quickly arrested and executed, as were most of his supporters. One was Charles Danvers, the man who been involved in the murder of Sir Henry Long more than six years earlier. Shakespeare's former patron, the Earl of Southampton, was also involved. He was imprisoned in the Tower of London rather than being put to death.

Elizabeth's suspicions naturally fell on the Globe Theatre and its actors. She sent some of her officers to question them about their involvement. They convinced her that they had staged the performance for the money Essex offered, not to help him overthrow her. They must have been convincing, because none were punished.

Later that year the Globe was the scene of Shakespeare's *The Tragedy of Hamlet, Prince of Denmark*. Many actors believe that Hamlet is the greatest theatrical role ever written for a man. The play contains what is Shakespeare's most famous soliloquy. It begins with the line, "To be or not to be, that is the question," (III. i. 57) and reveals Hamlet's complete despair.

Early in the play Hamlet realizes that the death of his beloved father was not accidental, as he had been led to believe. Rather, his father was murdered—by his uncle Claudius, who also married Hamlet's mother. Hamlet is horrified and wants revenge, yet it takes him most of the play to finally accomplish the deed. The delay likely is responsible for his own death as well as those of his uncle and mother—and several other characters as well.

A number of writers believe that *Hamlet* occupies a special niche among Shakespeare's works. As Greenblatt notes, "Hamlet marks a sufficient enough break in Shakespeare's career as to suggest some more personal cause. . . . A simple index of this transformation is the astonishing rush of new words, words that he had never used before in some twenty-one plays and in two long poems. There are, scholars have calculated, more than six hundred of these words, many of them not only new to Shakespeare but also new to the written record of the English language. This linguistic explosion seems to come not from a broadened vision of the world but from some shock or series of shocks to his whole life."[3]

One of these shocks was the ongoing grief from the death of his son Hamnet. Continually writing the name *Hamlet* must have been like continually picking at an open sore. The name was virtually identical to his son's.

Another factor was probably the near death of Southampton during Essex's ill-fated rebellion. Shakespeare was writing *Hamlet* during that period. It's likely that he still had fond memories of his time with the earl. The close questioning of the Lord Chamberlain's Men by the queen's agents in the wake of the rebellion would also have been upsetting. Had the agents determined that the troupe had been involved in the plot, Shakespeare and his friends would have suffered an immediate and very painful end.

Yet another factor was the death of Shakespeare's father in the late summer of 1601. It's likely that signs of his impending fate were evident while Shakespeare was working on the play. John Shakespeare was seventy, an especially advanced age for that era.

In short, it was a period when Shakespeare was surrounded by death. The ghost of Hamlet's father appears early in the play and advises Hamlet of his uncle's treachery. Most scholars believe that Shakespeare played the role. Rowe noted, "The top of his performance was the Ghost in his own *Hamlet*."[4]

The ghost says, "Pity me not, but lend thy serious hearing / To what I shall unfold." (I. v. 5–6) On one level, this speech serves to set the events of the play into motion. On another, deeper level, it may represent Shakespeare speaking to his audience. "Listen to me," he is telling the thousands of people in attendance. "I am about to bare my soul to you."

If that was his intention, he would not have needed to get in character. He would have been speaking straight from the heart.

Coming almost exactly at the middle of his dramatic career, *Hamlet* revealed just how far Shakespeare had come as a dramatist. As Anthony Holden notes, "In barely ten years he had already raised English drama from crude comedy, lumbering history and murderous melodrama to a level of intelligence, honesty, wit and humanity unmatched in any other era. . . . [*Hamlet*] has also been voted the 'masterwork' of the last thousand years, surpassing Michelangelo's Sistine Chapel, Beethoven's ninth symphony, the King James Bible, the Taj Mahal."[5]

Other Elizabethan Entertainments

The theater had to compete with many other forms of entertainment. Elizabethan citizens had a wide variety of choices for their free time.

Public executions usually drew huge crowds, in part because they were free. In a sense they were also plays. The "star" always came to a bad end. The most common form of execution was hanging. On other occasions the head of the offender would be chopped off. The worst fate awaited traitors, whose crimes were considered to be especially horrible. Sometimes they were partially hanged. Then they would be cut down, their stomachs sliced open and their intestines spilled out in front of them while they were still alive. Other times they would be drawn and quartered. Their shoulder and hip joints would be partially severed, then their arms and legs would be fastened to four horses, each one pointed in a different direction. The horses would be whipped and their efforts to run away would reduce the victim to a torso. Commonly their heads would be chopped off and put on pikes as a warning to others not to try the same thing.

Sometimes people would visit mental asylums. It was considered very enjoyable to watch the "antics" of the inmates.

Bear-baiting was another popular option. Captured bears would be starved to weaken them. Their claws would be removed. They would be attached by chains to heavy wooden posts in the middle of an arena. Dogs would attack them. The bears would kill or badly wound some dogs. The fallen dogs would quickly be replaced. Only rarely were the bears killed. Normally they would be wounded badly but allowed to recover. In the meantime, there were always fresh bears. The best ones were given names such as George Stone and Harry Hunks.

Sometimes bulls were substituted for bears. Breeders developed a special type of dog to attack bulls. They were bulldogs. They were larger than modern bulldogs. Many bit the bulls in the face or on its ears. Because they hung on as hard as they could, today a bulldog can mean someone who is tenacious.

A variation involved tying an ape to the back of a pony. People loved it. "To see the animal [the pony] kicking amongst the dogs, with the screams of the ape, beholding the curs [dogs] hanging from the neck and ears of the pony, is very laughable,"[6] wrote one obviously satisfied customer.

A number of villages and towns used bulls in an annual festivity. A bull would be released. The citizens would chase it, striking it with clubs. When they got tired of their "sport," they would beat the bull to death.

Other animals were often at risk. The nobility enjoyed hunting foxes and boars. They also used trained hawks to kill small birds. Among the common people, cockfights and dogfights were common.

An early form of soccer known as gameball was catching on. The same was true of shinty, an ancestor of hockey. Both were very violent. So were boxing and wrestling.

Other forms of recreation weren't as brutal. Tennis was popular among nobles and commoners. Nobles played in private indoor courts. Everyone else played in the streets or open fields. Tennis balls were stuffed with hair taken from poor women, who earned a little money for allowing it to be cut. Bowling, then known as skittles, was popular. Many people swam during the summer months. They might also play rounders, a primitive form of baseball.

Sometimes people just wanted a quiet night at home. They could play cards. Printing presses were churning out many books. A special favorite was *Foxe's Book of Martyrs*. It depicted—both in prose and vivid illustrations—the fate of Protestants during the reign of terror under "Bloody Mary."

The Burning of John Hooper, from *Foxe's Book of Martyrs*.

The presses also produced sheet music, which allowed families and larger groups to sing together. Many people played musical instruments. Dancing was also popular. Not everyone approved of the two sexes mingling so close to each other. One horrified onlooker referred to "the horrible vice of pestiferous dancing . . . what kissing and bussing [more kissing], what smooching and slabbering one of another."[7]

People could also play with their pets. Cats, dogs, monkeys, and birds were popular. Because fleas were very common in that era, many well-to-do people carried their pets in public. The fleas would hop from their human hosts onto the animal that was being carried.

King James VI of Scotland succeeded England's Queen Elizabeth in 1603. He became the patron of Shakespeare's troupe of actors. During his reign, he ordered a new translation of the Bible. Completed in 1611, it was called the King James Bible in his honor.

Chapter 7

The King's Men

Two years after *Hamlet* premiered, Queen Elizabeth died. In many cases in history, the death of a ruler with no children resulted in chaos. England didn't suffer the same fate. Elizabeth's thirty-seven-year-old nephew James became king. James was already king of Scotland, where he was known as James VI. Now he was James I of England.

There was a certain irony in this. Elizabeth's cousin Mary had married Henry Stuart of Scotland. Soon after Elizabeth became queen, Mary—now known as Mary Queen of Scots—put forth her claim to the English throne. Civil war threatened to break out. Mary was captured and imprisoned. Eventually Elizabeth ordered her to be executed.

Now Mary's son was taking what his family regarded as their proper right: the rule of England. Elizabeth had been a member of the Tudor family. Because she left no direct heirs, that line came to an end. James began the Stuart dynasty.

With his accession, the Lord Chamberlain's Men received an immediate benefit. James was concerned about the amount of power that Puritans held. Puritans disliked the theater, so he decided to promote theatrical productions. In particular, he promoted the Lord Chamberlain's Men and renamed them the King's Men. The name change was more than cosmetic. Under Elizabeth, the troupe had normally performed at court about three times each year. Under James, their new patron, that number quadrupled. They also continued to perform at the Globe as often as they could.

For Shakespeare, becoming a member of the King's Men conferred several benefits. It increased the prestige of the company and made him a king's servant, entitled to wear a red gown. It even gave him a title: He was now a Gentleman Groom of the Most Honourable Privy Council.

One of the first plays that the newly named troupe presented for the King was *Othello*. The play has a number of parallels with contemporary culture. There is racial tension because the hero (Othello) is a Moor, a black man. He marries a white woman named Desdemona. Iago, a white man, is angry at Othello. He claims his anger resulted from being passed over for a promotion by Othello, his commanding officer. Part of this anger is expressed in racial slurs. Iago calls Othello "thicklips" and "a barbary horse" and refers to his "sooty bottom."

Iago devotes most of his energy in trying to turn Othello against his wife. The process proves to be remarkably easy. Iago convinces Othello that Desdemona has been unfaithful him. Iago is lying. Desdemona has been faithful. Othello becomes almost physically sick with jealousy, and he smothers her.

The play also touches on homosexuality. Iago tells Othello that he was with Cassio, the character he has convinced Othello is his wife's lover. At one point, Iago says:

> [Cassio] laid his leg
> Over my thigh, and sigh'd and kiss'd, and, then,
> Cried "Cursed fate that gave thee to the Moor!" (III. iii. 429–431)

Again Iago is lying. He was never with Cassio in the way he describes.

Iago is not only the worst villain Shakespeare created but also one of the greatest villains in all of literature. Iago is also another name for James. Shakespeare must have felt very confident in himself to give such an evil man the same name as the king.

James may have laughed at the use of his name in the play, but in other areas he wasn't as self-confident. He was uneasy on his throne. His own father had been assassinated. His mother had been executed by Elizabeth. He had survived at least one attempt on his life. Underneath his royal robes, he wore heavy quilted underwear, the early seventeenth-century version of body armor. Today, it wouldn't stop a bullet, but back then it would have made it harder for someone to stick him with a knife.

That wasn't all. James himself was a published author. One of his most famous works was the *Daemonologie,* published in 1597. It expressed his belief in, and fear of, witchcraft. He was by no means alone in this belief. Many people in England felt the same way. Elizabeth had even referred to her cousin as a witch. In his book, James said that witches were allied with the Devil. They wanted to destroy the entire state. The obvious target, of course, was the king, the head of the state. James's fears become realized late in 1605, when the country was shaken to its roots by the discovery of the Gunpowder Plot. James had been the primary target. In March the following year, a rumor spread that James had been stabbed to death. The news—which he quickly denied—only made people more restless.

Shakespeare probably saw an opportunity to get on James's good side and also provide the country with assurances that it could survive in spite of all the uncertainty. Throughout his works, he depicted the horrible consequences of civic disorder. Legally, he couldn't write a play that referred directly to James. He decided to push the events far back in time. He would show that one of James's distant ancestors was a great and heroic man. The implication would be obvious: James was the same type of man.

The result was *Macbeth*. Because of the king's interest in witches, it isn't an accident that the play opens with three witches making up a gruesome potion. Soon Macbeth and his friend and fellow nobleman Banquo appear. The witches greet Macbeth, saying:

All hail, Macbeth! hail to thee, Thane [Lord] of Glamis!
All hail, Macbeth! hail to thee, Thane of Cawdor!
All hail, Macbeth, that shall be king hereafter. (I. iii. 48–50)

This apparently friendly greeting causes Macbeth to shudder. He is indeed Thane of Glamis. He has just defeated the traitorous Thane of Cawdor. He soon learns his reward: He is the new Thane of Cawdor as well. That makes the witches two-for-two. His shudder makes it apparent that he has also entertained fantasies of becoming king.

There is, of course, a problem. Scotland already has a king, whose name is Duncan. Duncan is popular among his people. He also has two sons to succeed him. Macbeth is not related to the king. There is only one way of realizing the third prophecy: murdering Duncan.

Banquo asks the witches what will happen to him. They shake their heads. He will never be a king, they tell him, but he will "beget kings." His descendents will rule Scotland.

Historically, Banquo's role as a "begetter of kings" seems to have been accurate. James could trace his ancestry back several centuries to Banquo. In a memorable scene in the play, Macbeth sees a vision of the future through a kind of magic mirror. It shows a number of kings. All are descended from Banquo. It is likely that when this scene was performed at court, an actor would have approached James with a mirror.

There were two problems with this rather obvious bit of flattery. One was that the real Macbeth was probably not as bad as Shakespeare made him out to be. While he did kill King Duncan (who was actually a young and ineffective leader), his rule afterward was not the reign of terror that Shakespeare portrays. In addition, Holinshed's *Chronicles of England, Scotland and Ireland* (an historical work published in 1577 and Shakespeare's primary source material) notes that Banquo was Macbeth's chief supporter in the crime.

Shakespeare knew he had to whitewash that part of the story. James would not be pleased at being identified with a family of regicides. In the play, Banquo is innocent of wrongdoing. Macbeth hires assassins to get rid of Banquo and his son Fleance. The murderers are only half successful. Banquo dies at their hands, but Fleance escapes. Macbeth is furious, but there is nothing he can do.

He becomes consumed by his guilt, as does his wife, Lady Macbeth. They feel they have to kill anyone who presents a threat to the throne. Both pay for their crimes. Lady Macbeth begins sleepwalking, obsessed with cleaning the blood that she believes stains her hands. "What, will these hands ne'er be clean?" she moans in her sleep. (V. i. 41). She dies not long afterward. Macbeth soon follows her in death. He is killed in battle. The play shows the darkness that lurks in the heart of every person.

Another story about the fall of a king was written soon afterward (some scholars believe that it actually preceded *Macbeth*). It was *King Lear*. Lear is an aging monarch who decides to divide up his kingdom among his three daughters. He explains that the amount of land each woman receives will depend on how much they say they love him. The two older daughters, Goneril and Regan, don't care for their father at all, but they are very greedy. They tell him a lot of lies about how much they care for him. The youngest daughter, Cordelia (her father's favorite), is disgusted. She refuses to kiss up. She pays dearly. She receives nothing.

Soon Lear discovers the truth. Goneril and Regan both treat him very poorly. In desperation, he flees to a barren heath in the middle of a horrible storm. By then, everything he had has been stripped away. His folly has reduced him to nothing. His only companion is his fool.

A play with most of the same characters had been presented in London about a decade earlier. It ended with Lear and Cordelia being reconciled. Shakespeare's play is different. He doesn't let the audience off happily. Cordelia is hanged. In his rage, Lear batters the executioner to death. He carries his daughter's body onto the stage:

> Howl, howl, howl, howl! O, you are men of stones.
> Had I your tongues and eyes, I'd use them so
> That heaven's vault should crack! She's gone for ever! . . .
>
> Why should a dog, a horse, a rat, have life,
> And thou no breath at all? Thou'lt come no more,
> Never, never, never, never, never. (V. iii. 258–260, 306–308)

Moments later, he dies.

Never again would Shakespeare write a tragedy with the same raw power as his Big Four: *Hamlet, Othello, Macbeth*, and *King Lear*. While *Lear* may have signaled the end of one phase of his playwriting, it marked the beginning of another. Biographer Anthony Holden points out that in *King Lear*, Shakespeare is "playing the real life father tragically deprived of his beloved son, and pouring all his paternal love, sharpened by years of guilty absenteeism, into his daughters. . . . The emphasis in *Lear* onwards is otherwise exclusively, almost obsessively, on daughters."[1]

Susanna was now twenty-two, while Judith was twenty. Both were ripe for marriage. With his own (very likely) unhappy marriage still on his mind, Shakespeare must have wanted something better for the two young women. One possible sign of this concern was the increasing amount of property he was buying in and around Stratford. In addition to New Place, he owned several other parcels. He may not have lived very much in Stratford, but his influence there was becoming increasingly pervasive.

As Holden continues, "Shakespeare had rebuilt his family fortunes. The residence in Henley Street now known as The Birthplace; the handsome spread flourishing around New Place, complete with full-time gardener; extensive landholdings within the town and all around it: This was an estate more than substantial enough to ensure his family's future. At the age of forty-one, he need never work again."[2]

But Shakespeare was nowhere near ready to retire.

Guy Fawkes and the Gunpowder Plot

When James succeeded Elizabeth on the throne, many English Catholics were optimistic about him. His mother, Mary Queen of Scots, had been Catholic, as had James's wife, Queen Anne of Denmark.

These hopeful Catholics were soon disappointed. While James wasn't as cruel as Elizabeth, he made it clear that he didn't like Catholics either. Within a year of coming to power, he introduced some laws that made their lives more difficult.

Led by a man named Robert Catesby, a small group of Catholics decided to take action. They concocted a plan to blow up the Parliament building when the king was attending the opening session. Nearly all of the most important men in the realm would also be there. The explosion would destroy the English government.

First they rented a house next to Parliament. One of the plotters, Guy Fawkes, lived there. They also rented a cellar that extended under the Parliament building. Slowly the men began sneaking gunpowder into the cellar. Eventually they had at least twenty barrels down there, hidden beneath several feet of wood and coal. According to the plan, Fawkes would light a fuse. It would be long enough to allow time for him to escape. Immediately after the explosion had devastated the Parliament building overhead, Catesby and the others planned to kidnap James's daughter Elizabeth and place her on the throne. She would simply be a figure-head. The plotters and other Catholic leaders would be the real rulers.

Midway through 1605, the kings' agents thought something was suspicious. They began tailing Fawkes, yet failed to uncover the plot.

On the night of October 26—just over a week before Parliament's scheduled opening on November 5—a Member of Parliament named Baron Monteagle received a mysterious note: "They shall receive a terrible blow this Parliament, and yet they shall not see who hurts them. The danger is passed as soon as you have burned the note."[3] Many scholars believe the note was written by Francis Tresham, one of the plotters. Monteagle was not only Tresham's brother-in-law but also a Catholic. Monteagle didn't burn the note. Instead he showed it to Robert Cecil, one of James's closest advisers. Cecil immediately brought the note to the king.

James already had personal experience with gunpowder. His father, Henry Stuart, had been murdered when a massive explosion ripped apart a house where he'd been staying. James and Cecil decided to wait until the last possible minute.

On the night of November 4—only hours before the opening—government agents raided the house and cellar. They found Fawkes making his final preparations, and they found the huge stash of gunpowder. Fawkes was arrested and tortured.

Word swiftly spread through the capital, and bonfires were lit early the following morning. The fires celebrated the deliverance of the country from terror.

The other plotters fled. They were quickly hunted down. Some were killed on the spot. Others were taken back to London for a highly publicized trial. Their deaths were especially gruesome. According to historian Bruce Robinson, "They would be hanged until half-dead, upon which their genitals would be cut off and burned in front of them. Still alive, their bowels and heart would be removed. Finally they would be decapitated and dismembered; their body parts would be publicly displayed, eaten by the birds as they decomposed."[4]

Rumors of more plots against the king continued to run rampant throughout the country. The ambassador from Venice wrote, ". . . the king is in terror. He does not appear nor does he take his meals in public as usual. . . . The Lords of the council are also are alarmed and confused by the plot itself and [by] the King's suspicions; the city is in great uncertainty; Catholics fear heretics, and vice-versa; both are armed, foreigners live in terror of their houses being sacked by the mob."[5]

The plot had long-lasting effects. New restrictions were placed on Catholics. One was losing the right to vote. It took more than two centuries before they regained it.

Today the English still mark Guy Fawkes Day on November 5 because of the disaster that was narrowly averted. Images of Fawkes and other conspirators are burned over roaring bonfires. The festivities conclude with a fireworks display.

Guy Fawkes kneels before King James I after being captured.

Shakespeare sits in his study, working on one of his plays. The open book near his right foot is perhaps one of his sources, such as Lord North's translation of Plutarch's *Lives* or Raphael Holinshed's *The Chronicles of England, Scotland, and Ireland*. Shakespeare consulted sources such as these for many of his plot details.

Chapter 8

Farewell to the Stage

While Shakespeare is most famous for the four great tragedies, he wrote other works at the same time. Several are classified as "problem plays": *Measure for Measure, All's Well That Ends Well,* and *Troilus and Cressida.* They aren't histories; they aren't tragedies; they might be comedies except that many parts just aren't very funny. The humor in the "funny parts" isn't the same lighthearted fun as in earlier comedies such as *As You Like It, Twelfth Night,* and *Midsummer Night's Dream.*

The end of this period also marked several important events in Shakespeare's personal life. His daughter Susanna married Dr. John Hall in 1607. From the available evidence, she chose very well. "In December 1607 the doctor's father, William Hall of Acton, made out a will in which the claims of an elder son were overlooked and John Hall as a younger son was named as his father's inheritor and 'sole executor,'" says biographer Park Honan. "The poet too appears to have trusted Hall above other men he knew."[1]

Shakespeare's brother Edmund, at age twenty-seven, died at the end of the year. He had followed his older brother into a theatrical career, but he was only marginally successful.

Susanna gave birth to a daughter, Elizabeth, early the following year. The tiny girl was Shakespeare's first grandchild. Mary Shakespeare lived just long enough to greet her great-grandchild. She died in September.

Around the time his mother died, Shakespeare's imagination received a fresh source of inspiration. The King's Men took advantage of their financial success to start up a second theater, known as the Blackfriars because the site was a former monastery.

Owning Blackfriars, which was the first indoor theater, enabled the King's Men to put on plays year round. During late spring, summer, and much of the fall, the weather was good enough for the Globe to be open. When foul weather forced it to close, Blackfriars would open.

The King's Men could charge much more for seeing performances at Blackfriars. Ticket prices restricted the audience to the wealthier members of the theatergoing public. For an even higher admission fee, a select few could sit on the stage. Having the audience so close was not always a good idea. One night, one of the "special guests" crossed the stage in front of an actor who was delivering an important speech. The actor snarled an insult at the man, who slapped him in retaliation. The other actors had to separate the two men before further damage could be done.

The theater's small size and intimate setting allowed it to be lit in the evenings by candlelight. The players could offer both daytime and evening performances. Blackfriars quickly turned out to be more profitable than the Globe. Referring to Blackfriars, a London auditor reported in 1612 that the troupe "got, and yet doth, more in winter in the said great hall by a thousand pounds than they were used to get on the Bankside [site of the Globe]."[2]

Shakespeare's final five plays—*Timon of Athens, Pericles, Cymbeline, The Winter's Tale,* and *The Tempest*—all premiered there. Called "romances," they were different from their predecessors. For one thing, Shakespeare was no longer writing for the groundlings. As Holden notes, the groundlings "liked their humor broad, their heroes princely and their action bloody."[3] In contrast, the Blackfriars audience was better educated, more sophisticated, and generally older than the groundlings. At the same time, Shakespeare wanted to move beyond tragedy. As a middle-aged man, he was more concerned with accepting things as they are. He was apparently feeling more mellow, more willing to see the good in life.

One particular emphasis was on different generations within broken families that manage to get together again. In *King Lear*, for example, a father and his daughters become violently separated. In these final plays, fathers and daughters are reunited. Many scholars speculate that this theme is based on Shakespeare's long separation from his own daughters. *The Winter's Tale* adds another dimension to the family theme. It concludes with a husband and wife getting together after many years of separation. It may have represented Shakespeare's own hopes.

In 1609, his sonnets were finally published as a collection. Most if not all of them had been written long before then. In all likelihood, they had been circulated privately among Shakespeare's friends with little or no expectation of becoming public. The reason for publishing them at this time might have had something to do with yet another outbreak of plague. It kept the theaters closed for more than a year, from the late summer of 1608 until the end of 1609. Seeing Shakespeare's work in print would have helped keep the public aware of him during this period, and sales of the collection may have brought him some extra income. The King's Men also stayed busy and profitable. Because of their special status as performers at his court, James provided the troupe with extra money "for their special practice in the time of infection."[4]

There is some controversy about the way in which the sonnets were published. Some scholars maintain that Shakespeare had decided the time was right. They suggest that since some of the sonnets have sexual overtones, he waited until his mother died before making them public. He didn't want to shock her with what he had written.

Sonnets were usually composed with someone particular in mind. Many of Shakespeare's seem to be addressed to a handsome young man. The first seventeen urge the young man to get married. More than a hundred of the poems that follow describe his physical beauty and how much the poet cares for him. Most of the final ones detail the poet's illicit love affair with a woman whom scholars term the "Dark Lady." A number of these have lines that are "R-rated" or even "X-rated."

The dedication to the collection is maddeningly imprecise:

> To the Onlie Begetter of
> These Insuing Sonnets
> Mr W. H. All Happiness
> And that Eternity
> Promised
> By
> Our Everliving Poet
> Wisheth
> The Well-wishing
> Adventurer in
> Setting forth
> T.T.

Scholars have long tried to identify the mysterious "Mr. W. H.," the man to whom Shakespeare was apparently addressing the dedication. Shakespeare knew several men with those initials. By reversing the order of the initials, the most notable becomes Henry Wriothesley, the Earl of Southampton. Shakespeare was probably staying with Wriothesley when he began writing the sonnets. At the time, Wriothesley was about twenty—and unmarried.

There is, however, an entirely different possibility. It involves a printer named Thomas Thorpe (the "T.T." at the end of the dedication). As author Peter Quennell observes, "Thorpe was an industrious businessman, who earned a livelihood by picking up manuscripts—there was then nothing that resembled a law of copyright to protect the unlucky author's claims—and either selling them to members of the book-trade or issuing them beneath his own imprint."[5] If this is true, Quennell continues, "Shakespeare himself probably was not consulted; clearly he did not correct the proofs; and almost certainly he had no share in framing the curious [dedication]."[6]

Under this interpretation—which a number of other respected Shakespeare biographers accept—the mysterious "Mr. W. H." has no connection with Shakespeare. Rather, he is simply William Hall, an otherwise obscure young man who somehow managed to get his hands on a copy of the sonnets. A "begetter" is a person who gives life to something. As Quennell concludes, "[Hall] had given the manuscript life by delivering it into a publisher's clutches."[7]

In 1610 Shakespeare began writing *The Tempest*. Some scholars believe it was written to mark his farewell to the stage. In this interpretation, one of the main characters, Prospero, speaks for Shakespeare himself. Prospero and his daughter Miranda have lived on an otherwise deserted island for many years. During this time, he has taught himself magic. Eventually, a group of people is washed ashore during a shipwreck. The group includes his brother, one of the men who deliberately stranded him on the island. Using his magic, Prospero orchestrates the events that follow. Near the end of the play, he describes how his magic has even influenced natural events:

> I have bedimmed
> The noontide sun, call'd forth the mutinous winds,
> And 'twixt the green sea and the azured vault
> Set roaring war. To the dread rattling thunder
> Have I given fire, and rifted Jove's stout oak

With his own bolt. The strong-based promontory
Have I made shake; and by the spurs pluck'd up
The pine and cedar. Graves at my command
Have waked their sleepers, oped, and let 'em forth
By my so potent art. (V. i. 41–50)

This is the same "magic" that the playwright, the director, and the actors use to create the illusion of the action that happens in the narrow confines of a theater. As Prospero continues, he declares it is time to hang up his "magic wand":

> But this rough magic
> I here abjure . . .
> I'll break my staff
> Bury it certain fathoms in the earth,
> And deeper than did ever plummet sound
> I'll drown my book. (V. i. 50–51, 54–57)

There was more. Shakespeare knew that audiences were an important part of the "magic." They had to believe what they were seeing on stage. A few scrawny trees had to represent an entire forest. A handful of men carrying fake swords had to stand for a massive army. Putting a costume on an actor transformed him from his "normal" self into a king, a nobleman, a citizen of Rome—or even a woman.

Theater was therefore a two-way street. It wasn't enough for Shakespeare to say he was leaving the stage. The audience had to let him go. In a brief epilogue, Prospero faces the audience and addresses it directly:

> But release me from my bands
> With the help of your good hands . . .
> As you from crimes would pardon'd be
> Let your indulgence set me free. (Epilogue, 9–10, 19–20).

One of the greatest careers in theatrical history was nearly over.

Source of *The Tempest*

The Tempest was likely inspired by an historic event that came soon after the English established a colony in Jamestown, Virginia, in 1607. From the start, the colony struggled. It desperately needed supplies and additional settlers. In early June 1609, nine ships set out from England and headed toward Jamestown. The vessels carried at least 500 people, making it the largest European colonizing expedition at that point in history.

In late July, a storm struck the fleet and scattered the ships. Seven of them managed to straggle into Jamestown. The eighth disappeared with all the people on board. The worried colonists believed that the same fate had struck the *Sea Venture*, the largest ship. One of the vessel's passengers was Sir George Somers, an important official in the Virginia Company, the group that had financed and organized the Jamestown colony. Another was Sir Thomas Gates, who had just been appointed the colony's governor.

As the weeks stretched on with no sign of the ship, the colonists gave up hope of ever seeing the vessel again. One of the ships carried the grim news back to England. There had been a great deal of interest in the expedition. Many people were dismayed to learn of the loss of the *Sea Venture*.

However, Somers, Gates, and the others hadn't drowned. The ship had been carried far off course. It began leaking. Crewmen desperately threw many pieces of equipment over the side to lighten the ship and keep it afloat. Then it struck a reef off Bermuda. The ship was wrecked, but all 150 people (and one dog) made it safely to shore.

The Bermudas had been known to mariners for several decades. One ship had even left some pigs behind to provide food for anyone who happened to be wrecked. The islands had a somewhat sinister reputation, with devils and other wicked spirits rumored to live there. If they did, they stayed away from the colonists. Using wood from trees on the island and parts salvaged from the wreckage of the *Sea Venture,* the colonists spent ten months building two new ships. They sailed to Jamestown in May 1610. The other colonists were overjoyed to see them.

A ship rushed back to England with the happy news. The seemingly miraculous survival of the *Sea Venture*'s colonists and crew created a sensation. Not surprisingly, several accounts were printed. One was *A Discovery of the Barmudas* by Sylvester Jourdain, who had been on the *Sea Venture*. It was followed by *A True Declaration of the Estate of the Colonie in Virginia*. A compilation of several documents, its main purpose was to assure the public that the Virginia Company was running a sound business.

The third account—and probably the most important to Shakespeare—was *The True Reportory of the Wrack, and Redemption of Sir Thomas Gates Knight*. While the author, William Strachey, didn't publish it until 1625, the account is dated July 15, 1610. Many scholars are convinced that Shakespeare read it soon afterward. The first recorded performance of *The Tempest* was on November 1, 1611. Shakespeare could have composed it during the one-year period between the fall of 1610 and the fall of 1611. These scholars also note that, although the play takes place on an island in the Mediterranean Sea rather than in Bermuda, much of the action in *The Tempest* is similar to what Strachey describes. Many lines seem to almost echo Strachey's own words.

The Tempest wasn't the only significant result from the voyage of the *Sea Venture*. One of the passengers was John Rolfe. His pregnant wife died on

John Rolfe marries Pocahontas.

Bermuda giving birth to their daughter, who also died. Not long after Rolfe arrived in Jamestown, he met Chief Powhatan's daughter Pocahontas and married her. Rolfe, Pocahontas, and their young son traveled to London in 1616 to raise additional interest in the colony. Pocahontas died early the following year.

After the wreck of the *Sea Venture*, the British government sent another expedition to colonize Bermuda. It has remained a British possession ever since, though for many years it has been self-governing.

Ben Jonson was one of Shakespeare's best friends. Born in 1572, he is most famous for his plays *Volpone* (*The Fox*) and *The Alchemist*. Jonson died in 1637.

Chapter 9

The Last Years

As patrons waited to enter the theater late in 1611 to see the first performance of *The Tempest*, they may well have discussed one of the year's most important events. Under the sponsorship of James I, a committee of scholars had retranslated the Old and New Testaments of the Bible. They called their translation the King James Bible.

Even if *The Tempest* was intended to mark Shakespeare's departure from the theater, it didn't. He began to collaborate with John Fletcher, a rising young London playwright One of the collaborations was *Two Noble Kinsmen*, which is rarely performed today. Another was *Cardenio*. Any copies of *Cardenio* disappeared long ago. Records indicate that the play was performed by the King's Men. A notation identifies Shakespeare and Fletcher as the authors. A third collaboration is known today as *Henry VIII*. It represents the logical conclusion to all the history plays Shakespeare had written earlier. *Henry VI, Part Three* ends with a marriage that unites the two primary families who had battled so long in civil war. The result of that marriage was Henry VII, who founded the Tudor House. Henry VIII was the son of Henry VII. Shakespeare couldn't write about Henry VIII while Elizabeth—his daughter and the last of the Tudor monarchs—was still alive.

Shakespeare and Fletcher didn't call their play *Henry VIII*. They called it *All Is True*. In the play, the most sympathetic character is Catherine, Henry's first wife. Henry is portrayed as a schemer.

Shakespeare may have been in attendance during what was literally an explosive performance at the Globe in 1613. As one spectator later recorded, "The kings players had a new play, called *All Is True*, set forth with many extraordinary circumstances of pomp and majesty. . . . Now . . . certain [cannons] being shot off . . . some of the paper, or other stuff, wherewith one of them was stopped [filled], did light upon the thatch [roof], where being thought at first but an idle smoke, and their eyes more attentive to the show, it kindled inwardly, and ran round like a train, consuming within less than an hour the whole house to the very grounds."[1]

The capacity crowd evacuated the burning building. No one was killed or even seriously injured.

The theater was rebuilt within a year. Shakespeare was no longer among the investors. By then, or soon afterward, he also sold off his interest in the Blackfriars, marking his true farewell to the theater.

His farewell to London probably came in the spring of 1615. The last record of his presence in the city dates from that time. He was one of seven men involved in a lawsuit regarding some property. Sometime after that, he returned to Stratford. He would never leave the town of his birth again.

It's likely that by then Shakespeare was in ill health. Early in 1616, he apparently became seriously ill. It may have been yet another outbreak of the plague, or it could have been typhoid fever, contracted by drinking polluted water from a stream near his home.

When Shakespeare drew up his will, he was very careful about the disposition of his considerable wealth. New Place went to his daughter Susanna and her husband, Dr. John Hall. They were also named as his executors. He took care of his daughter Judith and his surviving sister, Joan. There were bequests to other friends and relatives, and even a modest donation to the poor of Stratford.

There was nothing specific for his wife. Legally, it didn't matter. Under English law, she was automatically entitled to part of his estate. Still, as Stephen Greenblatt writes, "As a document charged with the remembering of friends and family in the final disposition of goods so carefully accumulated during a lifetime, Shakespeare's will—the last trace of his network of relationships—remains startling in its absolute silence in regard to his wife. In the will Shakespeare initially drafted, Anne Shakespeare was not mentioned at all; it is as if she had been completely erased."[2]

Perhaps under pressure from Susanna and her husband, Shakespeare made some changes in late March. He added something for Anne: his "second-best" bed. Some people see this somewhat unusual bequest as a final slap in the face to the wife with whom he had spent so little time. There may be other explanations. According to the custom of the times, a family's "best bed" was reserved for guests. The second-best was often the one that the husband and wife actually used. It may have been more comfortable, or perhaps it had belonged to Anne in the first place. It may have been a Hathaway family heirloom. If that were the case, Shakespeare was simply making sure she got it back.

In any event, biographer Anthony Holden disagrees with Greenblatt's interpretation. "Far from signifying the rottenness of their marriage, the bequest ["second-best bed"] suggests a specific (and rather touching) vote of thanks from a grateful husband, aware of his own shortcomings, for the long-suffering, dogged loyalty of a partner who had for years put up with a long-distance marriage, single-handedly brought up his children in his absence, and overlooked his own all-too-evident lapses when he did choose to put in the occasional appearance at home."[3]

His other daughter, Judith, had been married shortly before this new version. Shakespeare thought very little of her husband, Thomas Quiney. Judith was thirty-one, while Quiney was just twenty-seven. The couple was married during the season of Lent. They were supposed to get a special license to do that. Because they didn't, the church excommunicated them. Quiney's reputation was further dimmed when he confessed to fathering a child with another woman. His misdeeds provided another reason for Shakespeare to change his will. He didn't want to run the risk of Quiney getting his hands on Judith's inheritance.

According to one story, soon after Shakespeare drew up the final version of his will, his longtime friend playwright Ben Jonson came down from London to visit him. Poet Michael Drayton, a local man who was a patient of Shakespeare's son in law Dr. Hall, joined them for an evening of drinking and laughter. If it occurred, this little party may have done him in. As Anthony Burgess explains, "[Shakespeare] was, perhaps, not over-disposed to take care of himself. He may have drunk with abandon, encouraged by Ben, then sweated in a hot room, walking out hatless and cloakless to speed his guests on their way, pooh-poohed warnings of the danger of a chill April night. A quick attack of pneumonia . . . was enough to effect his quietus [death]."[4]

We do know the date of his death. It was April 23, which may have also been the date on which he was born. If so, he was exactly fifty-two.

He would become "not of an age, but for all time." But it wouldn't happen right away.

The King James Bible

By the time Elizabeth assumed the throne of England, several English versions of the Bible were in existence. The first one was handwritten by John Wycliffe in 1380. The organized church was furious. Its leaders wanted only Latin Bibles. They felt that the authority of clergymen would be undermined if people could read the Bible in their own language. The church's anger with Wycliffe didn't die when he did. Nearly half a century after his death, his bones were dug up, ground into powder, and thrown into a river. John Hus, one of Wycliffe's followers, was burned at the stake in 1415. Wycliffe Bibles were part of the fuel.

Beginning in 1517, Martin Luther's Protestant Reformation spurred even greater interest in English Bibles. The translators used a variety of sources, so the different Bibles contained significant differences. After Henry VIII broke away from the Catholic Church to found the Church of England, it seemed apparent that a single standard edition should be established for the new church. Henry didn't live long enough to accomplish that. Neither did Elizabeth.

Within a year of succeeding Elizabeth, James summoned dozens of church officials and scholars to a meeting. He wanted to settle the disagreements among the factions within the Church of England. It's not clear whether James had considered a new translation at this point, but a clergyman named John Reynolds did. According to Biblical scholar Dr. Laurence M. Vance, Reynolds "moved his Majesty, that there might be a new translation of the Bible, because those which were allowed in the reigns of Henry the eighth, and Edward the sixth, were corrupt and not answerable to the truth of the Original."[5]

James didn't need any prodding. He responded, "That a translation be made of the whole Bible, as consonant as can be to the original Hebrew and Greek; and this to be set out and printed, without any marginal notes, and only to be used in all churches of England in time of divine service."[6]

By July 1604, a committee of nearly fifty men was at work. James took pains to select men for their ability with language, for their ability as translators, and as we might say today, for their ability to "check their egos at the door." They all had to be willing to work together. The Bible was far too important to reflect one man's opinions.

The men were divided into six groups. Each group was assigned a different part of the Bible. They worked rapidly. Within four years, their joint efforts resulted in a preliminary draft. Not surprisingly, a few errors crept in. Perhaps the most famous involves the flight of Moses and the Hebrews out of Egypt toward the Promised Land. According to a Greek translation of the Hebrew, which they were also working with, the fugitives crossed the Red Sea. Such a route would have involved a substantial detour for a group trying to escape. In addition, the Red Sea itself is 150 miles wide. It would have taken a long time for a group on foot to cover such a distance. The original Hebrew appears to solve these problems. It simply says "Reed Sea," which suggests a smaller and shallower body of water. It would have been much closer to the most logical route away from Egypt.

Six of the original forty-seven men then spent nearly a year in London making further revisions. At that point, two of them—Myles Smith and Thomas Bilson—arranged a final draft for the printer. The King James Version of the Bible was published in 1611. The first ones were very large. They were chained to the pulpits of churches. Then smaller versions were printed, allowing many people to have their personal copies.

The King James Version became the accepted translation of the Christian Bible for nearly three centuries. Late in the nineteenth century, a new translation, the Standard Version, was introduced. Several other translations were produced

James Tissot's painting of St. Mark

during the twentieth century, including the Revised Standard, the New Revised Standard, and other versions. Each one used language that was considered more up to date and therefore easier to understand than the previous versions.

Not everyone agrees with this approach. Many people still prefer the King James Version. They maintain that it contains some of the finest poetry in the English language. Many believe that it is closer to the Bible as it was originally written.

MR. WILLIAM
SHAKESPEARES
COMEDIES,
HISTORIES, &
TRAGEDIES.

Published according to the True Originall Copies.

Martin Droeshout sculpsit London.

LONDON
Printed by Isaac Iaggard, and Ed. Blount. 1623.

This image of Shakespeare appeared on the cover of his collected plays in 1623. The artist, Martin Droeshout, was only fifteen when Shakespeare died and almost certainly had never seen him in person. He probably worked with some of Shakespeare's friends to develop this portrait, or he might have copied an existing portrait.

Chapter 10

Shakespeare's Legacy

"Spring, 1616," writes Shakespeare scholar Jonathan Bate. "The most brilliant dramatic talent of the age is no more. A man who came to youthful fame with a witty and erotic narrative poem taken from the classical mythology of Ovid. Who wrote occasional verse but found his true vocation in the theatre. . . . He has written for the leading acting company of the age, the King's Men. . . . There is only one place to lay such a man: in Westminster Abbey [the burial place of many of England's most famous people] close to the tombs of Geoffrey Chaucer, father of English verse, and Edmund Spenser, greatest poet of the Elizabethan age. . . . The triumvirate of English genius is complete."[1]

Anyone looking for Shakespeare's burial place in Westminster Abbey won't find it there. Bate isn't referring to Shakespeare. He is referring to Francis Beaumont, another poet and playwright. Beaumont died at age thirty-two, six weeks before Shakespeare. His death far overshadowed Shakespeare's in London's theatrical world. Beaumont was in the prime of his career. He had already replaced his predecessor in public acclaim. Shakespeare hadn't written anything for several years. He was yesterday's news. His body lies in a much more modest grave, in Stratford's Holy Trinity Church, where he had been baptized.

Shakespeare's direct line quickly disappeared. Judith and Thomas Quiney had three children. All died without leaving any heirs.

When Susanna Hall died in 1649 at the age of sixty-six, people still remembered her father. Her tombstone read, in part:

Witty above her sexe, but that's not all,

Wise to salvation was good Mistris Hall.

Something of Shakespeare was in that.[2]

Her daughter Elizabeth, who was eight years old at the time of her grandfather's death, became the only surviving heir. She was married twice but had no children. By the time she died in 1670, it's probable that most of Shakespeare's earthly goods had vanished.

Under most circumstances, his works could have suffered the same fate. Some plays had been printed during his lifetime. Others hadn't. When he died, no one had thought of printing an entire collection of a playwright's labors. It's possible that Shakespeare may not have cared what happened to his plays.

Two of his contemporaries, John Heminges and Henry Condell, thought differently. They spent several years collecting his plays, then published what became known as the *First Folio* in 1623. It is the main source today of Shakespeare's works. The book included an engraving of Shakespeare, the only firmly established image of him.

"We have but collected them [the plays], and done an office to the dead . . . without ambition either of self-profit or fame, only to keep the memory of so worthy a friend and fellow alive as was our Shakespeare. . . . And there we hope, to your diverse capacities, you will find enough both to draw and hold you; for his wit can no more lie hid than it could be lost,"[3] they wrote in the preface.

Despite their disclaimer, Heminges and Condell may have been motivated less by admiration than by practical considerations. Having all of Shakespeare's works together would make it easier to present them in the future.

Shakespeare's plays were frequently performed during the next century and a half, but he was far from the only deceased playwright whose works lived on. The name "William Shakespeare" didn't have the overtones that we associate with it today.

That situation changed with a famous actor named David Garrick, who began staging revivals of Shakespeare's works. Because of Garrick's influence and efforts, Shakespeare went from being "a bard" (another word for poet) to "The Bard" (the greatest poet of all time).

Even with this enormous change in attitude, not everyone has admired Shakespeare. Poet Samuel Taylor Coleridge, who wrote *The Rime of the Ancient Mariner*, said, "I believe Shakespeare was not a whit more intelligible in his own day than he is now to an educated man, except for a few local allusions of no consequence. He is of no age—nor any religion, or party or profession."[4]

George Bernard Shaw, a famous playwright, added, "With the single exception of Homer, there is no eminent writer . . . whom I can despise so entirely as I despise Shakespeare when I measure my mind against his. . . . It would positively be a relief to me to dig him up and throw stones at him."[5]

Even his close friend Ben Jonson—who praised him extensively after his death—put in a few harsh words. Writing apparently came easily to Shakespeare—so easily, in fact, that Jonson commented, "The Players have often mentioned it as an honor to Shakespeare that in his writing, whatsoever he penned, he never blotted out a line."[6] (Realistically, this cannot be true. Any writer constantly revises his or her work before releasing it.) Jonson continued, "Would [I wish] he had blotted a thousand [lines]."[7]

There is a different type of criticism. Some scholars believe that Shakespeare *wasn't* Shakespeare. According to this view, he couldn't have written such a wide variety of plays because of his limited background. Only a man with a university education who had also traveled widely could have written them, these critics say. Therefore someone besides William Shakespeare wrote the plays that are credited to him. It follows that whoever this person was simply used Shakespeare—a real person with very little talent—as a front man. Shakespeare happily accepted what must have been a substantial payoff to claim authorship. Most people who believe in an alternative Shakespeare are serious. They have written books and formed societies of like-minded individuals. The doubters include such heavyweights as *Tom Sawyer* author Mark Twain.

The earliest and probably the still most famous "substitute Shakespeare" was Sir Francis Bacon, a man of especially broad learning. Besides his vast knowledge, some of the evidence for his authorship comes from his letters and other writings. For example, a 1603 letter that he wrote to a friend concludes: "So desiring you to be good to concealed poets, I continue, yours very assured, Fr. Bacon."[8] His advocates contend that identifying himself in the category of "concealed poets" is a reference to himself as the "real" Shakespeare.

Humorist Ellis Parker Butler pokes fun at the Baconians. He describes a "visit" to a Stratford restaurant, where he requests ham and eggs. The waitress replies that the ham has all been eaten. She offers to substitute a "ham omelette." She adds, "Or some bacon, sir."

Butler is "convinced" that the waitress is trying to convey a coded message to him. Dropping the syllable *ome-* from *ham omelette* gives *Hamlette*, another spelling of the

95

famous Shakespearean character. The waitress seems to be pushing him in the direction of bacon. Butler further observes that she concludes each sentence with the word *sir*. "Why did the serving maid utter the word 'sir' three times?" he continues. "Evidently but to emphasise it. 'Sir—sir—sir!' Sir what? Sir Bacon! In other words, she was telling me that Sir Bacon was the author of Hamlet. I was immediately convinced."[9]

Another frequently mentioned candidate for "Shakespeare" is the Earl of Oxford. The idea seems to have two serious handicaps. One is that he apparently wasn't very fluent in Latin, which the author of the plays clearly was. Another is that he died in 1604. His advocates have a hard time explaining how he could have managed to write plays that didn't premiere for nearly a decade afterward.

The most intriguing alternate author is Christopher Marlowe. The problem is that Marlowe died in 1593 in a tavern brawl. At that point, Shakespeare had just begun his career. He continued writing plays for twenty more years. For Marlowe believers, the explanation is simple: Marlowe didn't die in 1593. In addition to his playwriting, he was involved in the treacherous world of Elizabethan-era politics. At the time of his "death," his supporters continue, he was about to face criminal charges that carried the death penalty. Citing alleged discrepancies in his death certificate and other documentation, they believe that his death was faked. Safely hidden far away from London, he wrote the great plays.

More recently, the Earl of Neville has been proposed. According to a book published in 2005, Neville, a distant relative of Shakespeare's who was imprisoned for his part in the Earl of Essex's short-lived revolt, "was well-educated, had traveled to all the countries used as settings in the plays and had a life that matched up with what 'Shakespeare' was writing about at the time."[10]

Most Shakespeare scholars reject the alternate author theory. There is no evidence that people who knew Shakespeare doubted that he wrote the plays credited to him. He was very well known. If there was another author, it would have required a vast cover-up involving dozens of people. Yet no one "blew the whistle," not even on his deathbed.

Bate is one of Shakespeare's defenders. He observes that Shakespeare was hardly a country bumpkin with limited knowledge. "Elizabethan grammar schools were very good," he points out. "They put our high schools to deep shame."[11]

Roger Pringle, director of the Shakespeare Birthplace Trust, takes the argument even further: "Like most previous theories that challenge Shakespeare's authorship of the plays, this claim makes the mistake of assuming his education and general knowledge of the world were very limited. There is plenty of evidence to suggest Shakespeare received a thoroughly good classical education at the Stratford grammar school and then, for well over 20 years, was involved in artistic and intellectual circles in London."[12]

Bate believes there is a deeper reason at work in seeking another author. It is a form of snobbery. "When Shakespeare became God [so to speak], some of his more ardent admirers started finding his life too dull and provincial," he writes. "They set about the hunt for a mystery, the search for a suitably glamorous alternative candidate. . . . We'll never find an alternative candidate for the authorship, since the plain fact of the matter is that Shakespeare did write the plays."[13]

Biographer Peter Quennell adds, "I have become firmly convinced that Shakespeare's plays and poems were produced, not by Derby, Oxford, Bacon, nor even by Christopher Marlowe after his supposed death, but by a middle-class writer born in Warwickshire in April 1564, and that all the current anti-Stratfordian theories involve some serious distortions of the facts."[14]

The argument that he didn't have enough learning to write about many things cuts both ways. Passage after passage reveals a deep and thorough understanding of the way that common people lived during his era. A nobleman, isolated from "real life" by servants and other people that do his bidding, couldn't have known or written about such matters as accurately and sympathetically as Shakespeare does. In addition, knowledge gained primarily from books does not guarantee artistic success. In fact, it may even work against it. Artists need to have a vivid imagination. Many successful scholars willingly concede that their imaginations are very limited.

There is another argument. Many people say that an author has to have firsthand experience of something to write well about it, but this is not true. For example, novelist Stephen Crane was never involved in an actual battle, yet many people regard his novel *The Red Badge of Courage* as one of the best depictions of the feelings that soldiers go through while they are fighting.

The question of the authorship of Shakespeare's plays likely will never be answered with certainty. However, there is at least one certainty: Somewhere in the world, someone is enjoying the works of William Shakespeare or using a word or phrase that he introduced into the English language.

The Shakespeare Jubilee

For more than 150 years after Shakespeare's death, his plays continued to be performed, but there was very little interest in him in Stratford. David Garrick, a famous eighteenth-century actor, was the man most responsible for changing that situation and elevating Shakespeare to his "superstar" status today.

Garrick was born in London in 1717. As a young man he was a wine merchant, but the business wasn't very successful. He soon became interested in the theater. At first he wrote and reviewed plays. He made his first appearance as an actor in March 1741, using an assumed name. He was virtually an overnight success. He became so well known and well regarded that by December he began appearing under his own name. He continued acting for the next twenty-five years. He also became a famous theatrical producer.

One of the main reasons for his success was his "naturalistic" acting. At that time, the style was to overact, using elaborate gestures. Garrick, in contrast, acted as normal people would. Most of his best roles were in plays that Shakespeare had written. He wasn't silent in his praise of his favorite playwright.

In 1767, the city fathers of Stratford wanted to rebuild city hall. They also wanted to include a statue of their favorite son, William Shakespeare, near the front door. They asked Garrick if he could help out.

Garrick was happy to oblige. He suggested a festival that would honor Shakespeare—and, not coincidentally, Stratford. Garrick was not the kind of man who did things halfway. He wanted what he called the Shakespeare Jubilee to be the finest outdoor festival England had ever seen. In addition to performing the works of Shakespeare, the event would include elaborate parades, fancy dress balls, and of course fireworks. In addition, everyone who attended would have the "privilege" of buying Shakespeare-themed merchandise at vastly inflated prices. In essence, the town of Stratford would become a three-day theme park.

Garrick knew how to work the press. For months prior to the opening in September 1769, newspapers were filled with breathless accounts of what those who made the trek to Stratford could expect to see and hear.

Unfortunately, the weather failed to cooperate. It rained heavily during the festival. People grimly joked that the town should change its name from Stratford-upon-Avon to Stratford-under-Avon. There weren't any opportunities to stage Shakespeare's plays. In fact, not a single line from any of his works was performed. Most of the other events also had to be canceled. As a result, Garrick's dramatic recitation of his poem "Ode upon dedicating a building and, erecting a statue, to Shakespeare, at Stratford-upon-Avon" became the centerpiece of the festival. It culminated in the lines "'Tis he! 'tis he! / The god of our idolatry."[15]

In terms of what had gone before, this praise was way over the top. Even Ben Jonson had admired Shakespeare "on this side of Idolatry."[16]

It didn't matter. Others soon took up Garrick's refrain. Shakespeare was transformed from a competent, well-regarded and very successful playwright into something entirely different.

"'After God,' proclaimed the nineteenth-century French author Alexandre Dumas, 'Shakespeare created most,'" comments Jonathan Bate. "Shakespeare has become the supreme deity not just of poetry or drama but of high culture itself."[17]

David Garrick and his wife, Eva Marie, painted by William Hogarth, 1757

Today, Stratford and many other cities and towns throughout the world stage annual Shakespeare festivals. Stratford is firmly on the map, as is its most famous citizen.

Garrick died in 1779. He was buried in Westminster Abbey in London, the final resting place for many English notables. Near the tomb, a short poem marks the enduring connection between Garrick and Shakespeare:

To paint fair nature by divine command,
Her magic pencil in her glowing hand.
A Shakespear rose: then, to expand his fame,
Wide o'er this breathing world, a Garrick came.
Though sunk in death the forms the Poet drew,
The actor's genius bade them breath anew;
Though, like the bard himself, in night they lay,
Immortal Garrick call'd them back to day;
And till eternity with pow'r sublime,
Shall mark the mortal hour of hoary time:
Shakespear and Garrick like twin-stars shall shine,
And earth irradiate with a beam divine.[18]

99

Chronology

1564	Born, probably on April 23, in Stratford-upon-Avon, England
1569–1570	Probably attends petty school in Stratford
1571–1572	Probably attends King's New School
1575	Possibly sees Queen Elizabeth when she visits Kenilworth Castle
1582	Marries Anne Hathaway
1583	Birth of daughter Susanna
1585	Birth of twins, daughter Judith and son Hamnet
1587	Possibly moves to London
1592	At least one of the Henry VI plays is performed in London
1593	Publishes *Venus and Adonis*
1594	Publishes *The Rape of Lucrece*; helps to found the Lord's Chamberlain's Men
1596	Son Hamnet dies; father, John Shakespeare, is granted a coat of arms
1597	Buys New Place, a home in Stratford
1599	Helps construct Globe Theatre and receives a share of the profits
1601	Father dies
1607	Daughter Susanna marries Dr. John Hall
1608	Granddaughter Elizabeth Hall is born; mother dies; helps acquire Blackfriars Theatre
1609	*The Sonnets* is published
1615	Probably leaves London for the last time, after being involved in a lawsuit
1616	Prepares will; daughter Judith marries Thomas Quiney; dies in Stratford, probably on April 23
1623	*First Folio* is published; Anne Shakespeare dies
1670	Shakespeare's granddaughter Elizabeth dies, which ends his direct line of descendants

Selected Works

With a few exceptions, there is no agreement among scholars about the exact dates when Shakespeare wrote his works or the precise order in which he wrote them. The following list is drawn from several sources and gives a general guide to his development.

PLAYS

The Two Gentlemen of Verona, 1587–92

The Tragedy of Titus Andronicus, 1587–92

Henry VI, Part Two, 1587–92

Henry VI, Part Three, 1587–92

Henry VI, Part One, 1587–92

The Taming of the Shrew, 1590–03

The Tragedy of King Richard III, 1592

The Comedy of Errors, 1593–94

Love's Labour's Lost, 1593–94

The Tragedy of Romeo and Juliet, 1594–95

Midsummer Night's Dream, 1594–95

Merchant of Venice, 1594–96

Richard II, 1595

The Life and Death of King John, 1595–97

Henry IV, Part One, 1596–97

Henry IV, Part Two, 1597–98

The Merry Wives of Windsor, 1598–99

Much Ado About Nothing, 1598–99

The Life of Henry V, 1599

The Tragedy of Julius Caesar, 1599

As You Like It, 1599–1600

Twelfth Night (What You Will), 1600

The Tragedy of Hamlet, Prince of Denmark, 1600–01

The Tragedy of Troilus and Cressida, 1601–02

All's Well That Ends Well, 1602–03

Measure for Measure, 1604

The Tragedy of Othello, the Moor of Venice, 1604

The Tragedy of Macbeth, 1606

The Tragedy of King Lear, 1606

The Tragedy of Antony and Cleopatra, 1606–07

The Tragedy of Coriolanus, 1607–08

Timon of Athens, 1607–08

Pericles, 1607–08

Cymbeline, 1609–10

The Winter's Tale, 1610–11

The Tempest, 1610–11

The History of Cardenio*, 1612

King Henry VIII (All Is True)*, 1612–13

The Two Noble Kinsmen*, 1613–14

  *With John Fletcher

POETRY

Venus and Adonis, 1592

The Rape of Lucrece, 1593–94

Sonnets, 1593–1600 (published 1609)

The Passionate Pilgrim, 1599

The Phoenix and the Turtle, 1601

A Lover's Complaint, 1609 (published in conjunction with *Sonnets*)

Timeline in History

1415 Outnumbered, exhausted English army commanded by Henry V defeats the French at the Battle of Agincourt.

1421 Henry VI is born.

1471 Henry VI dies.

1491 The future King Henry VIII is born.

1509 Henry VIII assumes the throne; marries Catherine of Aragon.

1517 Clergyman Martin Luther begins the Protestant Reformation.

1533 Henry VIII marries Anne Boleyn; the future Queen Elizabeth is born.

1536 Henry VIII executes Anne Boleyn.

1547 Henry VIII dies; his son Edward VI becomes king.

1553 Edward VI dies; Henry VIII's daughter Mary becomes queen.

1558 Mary dies; Elizabeth becomes Queen of England.

1564 Playwright Christopher Marlowe and Italian scientist Galileo Galilei are born; sculptor and painter Michelangelo dies.

1572 Playwright Ben Jonson is born.

1576 James Burbage builds first theater in more than 2,000 years.

1577 Raphael Holinshed publishes *The Chronicles of England, Scotland and Ireland*, which becomes the source for many of Shakespeare's plays; English seafarer Francis Drake begins voyage around the world in his ship, the *Golden Hind*.

1588 The English defeat the Spanish Armada.

1593 Christopher Marlowe is murdered.

1603 Queen Elizabeth dies; James VI of Scotland becomes James I of England.

1607 English colonists found Jamestown, the first English settlement in the New World.

1611 King James Version of the Bible is published.

1620 Puritans from England found Massachusetts Bay Colony.

1637 Ben Jonson dies.

1642 English Civil War begins; Puritans order theaters in England to be closed.

1660 Theaters in England are reopened.

1661 Playwright William D'Avenant opens his new Lincoln's Inn Fields Theatre in London with a production of *Hamlet*.

Chapter Notes

Chapter 1
A Story of Love and Death

1. Anthony Burgess, *Shakespeare* (New York: Penguin Books, 1972), p. 133.

2. Wiltshire County Council—Wiltshire Community History, http://www.wiltshire.gov.uk/community/getprinted.php?id=333

3. Stephen Greenblatt, *Will in the World: How Shakespeare Became Shakespeare* (New York: W. W. Norton, 2004), p. 339.

4. Burgess, p. 361.

5. Michael Wood, *Shakespeare* (New York: Basic Books, 2003), p. 342.

Chapter 2
A Boyhood in the Countryside

1. Peter Quennell, *William Shakespeare: A Biography* (Cleveland, Ohio: World Publishing Company, 1963), p. xiii.

2. Park Honan, *Shakespeare: A Life* (New York: Oxford University Press, 1998), p. 358.

3. Anthony Holden, *William Shakespeare: An Illustrated Biography* (Boston: Little Brown and Company, 2002), p. 34.

4. Anthony Burgess, *Shakespeare* (New York: Penguin Books, 1972), p. 32.

5. Peter Ackroyd, *Shakespeare: The Biography* (New York: Doubleday, 2005), pp. 68-69

Chapter 3
Love and Marriage

1. Dennis Kay, *Shakespeare: His Life, Work, and Era* (New York: William Morrow, 1992), p. 56.

Chapter 4
The Lost Years

1. Anthony Holden, *William Shakespeare: An Illustrated Biography* (Boston: Little Brown and Company, 2002), p. 122.

2. Park Honan, *Shakespeare: A Life* (New York: Oxford University Press, 1998), p. 92.

Chapter 5
Into (and out of?) London

1. Stephen Greenblatt, *Will in the World: How Shakespeare Became Shakespeare* (New York: W. W. Norton, 2004), p. 150.

2. Anthony Holden, *William Shakespeare: An Illustrated Biography* (Boston: Little Brown and Company, 2002), p. 103.

3. Liza Picard, *Elizabeth's London: Everyday Life in Elizabethan London* (New York: St. Martin's Press, 2003), p. 151.

4. Peter Ackroyd, *Shakespeare: The Biography* (New York: Doubleday, 2005), p. 111.

5. Ibid.

6. Holden, p. 118.

7. Picard, p. 217.

8. Ibid., p. 48.

9. Carl Hartman, "Shopping for luxuries in Shakespeare's time — oh, for a damasked pair of spurs!" The Associated Press, October 25, 2005. http://seattletimes.nwsource.com/html/nationworld/2002581474_shopping25.html

10. Ibid.

11. Peter Ackroyd, *London: The Biography* (New York: Doubleday, 2000), p. 68.

12. Samuel Pepys, *The Diary of Samuel Pepys,* http://www.blackmask.com/books24c/pepys.htm

13. Ibid.

14. Ibid.

Chapter 6
The Globe Theatre

1. Stephen Greenblatt, *Will in the World: How Shakespeare Became Shakespeare* (New York: W. W. Norton, 2004), p. 79.

2. Michael Wood, *Shakespeare* (New York: Basic Books, 2003), p. 226.

3. Greenblatt, pp. 307–308.

4. Ibid., p. 322.

5. Anthony Holden, *William Shakespeare: The Man Behind the Genius* (New York: Little Brown and Company, 1999), p. 191.

6. Greenblatt, p. 177.

7. Liza Picard, *Elizabeth's London: Everyday Life in Elizabethan London* (New York: St. Martin's Press, 2003), p. 215.

Chapter 7
The King's Men

1. Anthony Holden, *William Shakespeare: The Man Behind the Genius* (New York: Little Brown and Company, 1999), p. 224.

2. Ibid., p. 225.

3. Anthony Burgess, *Shakespeare* (New York: Penguin Books, 1972), p. 226.

4. Bruce Robinson, "The Gunpowder Plot," http://www.bbc.co.uk/history/state/monarchs_leaders/gunpowder_robinson_01.shtml

5. Stephen Greenblatt, *Will in the World: How Shakespeare Became Shakespeare* (New York: W.W. Norton, 2004), p. 337.

Chapter 8
Farewell to the Stage

1. Park Honan, *Shakespeare: A Life* (New York: Oxford University Press, 1998), p. 358.

2. Michael Wood, *Shakespeare* (New York: Basic Books, 2003), p. 333.

3. Anthony Holden, *William Shakespeare: An Illustrated Biography* (Boston: Little Brown and Company, 2002), p. 266.

4. Dennis Kay, *Shakespeare: His Life, Work, and Era* (New York: William Morrow, 1992), p. 356.

5. Peter Quennell, *William Shakespeare: A Biography* (Cleveland, Ohio: World Publishing Company, 1963), p. 122.

6. Ibid.

7. Ibid., p. 124.

Chapter 9
The Last Years

1. Michael Wood, *Shakespeare* (New York: Basic Books, 2003), p. 333.

2. Stephen Greenblatt, *Will in the World: How Shakespeare Became Shakespeare* (New York: W. W. Norton, 2004), p. 145.

3. Anthony Holden, *William Shakespeare: An Illustrated Biography* (Boston: Little Brown and Company, 2002), p. 322.

4. Anthony Burgess, *Shakespeare* (New York: Penguin Books, 1972), p. 259.

5. Dr. Laurence Vance, "A Brief History of the King James Bible." http://www.av1611.org/kjv/kjvhist.html

6. Ibid.

Chapter 10
Shakespeare's Legacy

1. Jonathan Bate, "Scenes from the Birth of a Myth and the Death of a Dramatist," in Stephanie Nolen, *Shakespeare's Face: Unraveling the Legend and History of Shakespeare's Mysterious Portrait* (New York: Free Press, 2002), p. 107.

2. Michael Best, "Married Life," *Shakespeare's Life and Times* (Internet Shakespeare Editions, University of Victoria: Victoria, BC, 2001–2005), http://ise.uvic.ca/Library/SLTnoframes/life/children.html

3. Michael Wood, *Shakespeare* (New York: Basic Books, 2003), p. 342.

4. "Views on Shakespeare Through the Ages," http://www.bbc.co.uk/education/asguru/english/08shakespeare/39biogandcontext/shakecontext02.shtml

5. Ibid.

6. Stephen Greenblatt, *Will in the World: How Shakespeare Became Shakespeare* (New York: W. W. Norton, 2004), p. 189.

7. Ibid.

8. "Summary of Baconian Evidence for Shakespeare Authorship," http://www.sirbacon.org/links/evidence.htm

9. Ellis Parker Butler, "Shakespeare-Bacon Controversy Solved," http://www.ellisparkerbutler.info/epb/biblio.asp?id=2358

10. Jenn Wiant, "Shakespeare's latest ghost writer is now purported to be Sir Henry Neville," Associated Press, October 20, 2005, http://seattlepi.nwsource.com/theater/245149_shakespearedebate20.html

11. Nolen, p. 116.

12. Wiant.

13. Nolen, p. 125.

14. Peter Quennell, *William Shakespeare: A Biography* (Cleveland, Ohio: World Publishing Company, 1963), p. xiii.

15. Stanley Wells, "The God of Our Idolatry," in Stephanie Nolen, *Shakespeare's Face: Unraveling the Legend and History of Shakespeare's Mysterious Portrait* (New York: Free Press, 2002), p. 25.

16. Ibid., p. 103.

17. Ibid.

18. *David Garrick's Life*, http://www.lichfieldgarrick.com/site/scripts/module.php?webSectionID=16&webSubSectionID=8

Further Reading

For Young Adults

Beneduce, Ann Keay. *William Shakespeare: The Tempest*. New York: Philomel Books, 1996.

Birch, Beverly. *Shakespeare's Tales*. London: Hodder Junior Books, 2002.

Chrisp, Peter. *Shakespeare*. New York: DK Publishing, 2002.

Coville, Bruce. *William Shakespeare's A Midsummer Night's Dream*. New York: Dial Books, 1996.

_____. *William Shakespeare's Romeo and Juliet*. New York: Dial Books, 1999.

_____. *William Shakespeare's Twelfth Night*. New York: Dial Books, 2003.

Garfield, Leon. *Shakespeare Stories*. Boston: Houghton Mifflin, 1998.

_____. *Shakespeare Stories II*. Boston: Houghton Mifflin, 2000.

Greenhill, Wendy, and Paul Wignall. *Shakespeare: Man of the Theater*. Chicago, Heinemann Library, 1999.

Ryan, Patrick. *Shakespeare's Storybook: Folk Tales That Inspired the Bard*. New York: Barefoot Books, 2001.

Stanley, Diane, and Peter Vennema. *Bard of Avon: The Story of William Shakespeare*. New York: Morrow Junior Books, 1992.

Thomas, Jane Resh. *Behind the Mask: The Life of Queen Elizabeth*. New York: Clarion Books, 1998.

Works Consulted

Ackroyd, Peter. *London: The Biography*. New York: Doubleday, 2000.

_____. *Shakespeare: The Biography*. New York: Doubleday, 2005.

Burgess, Anthony. *Shakespeare*. New York: Penguin Books, 1972.

Fallon, Robert Thomas. *How to Enjoy Shakespeare*. Chicago: Ivan R. Dee, 2005.

Greenblatt, Stephen. *Will in the World: How Shakespeare Became Shakespeare*. New York: W. W. Norton, 2004.

Hill, Wayne F., and Cynthia J. Öttchen. *Shakespeare's Insults: Educating Your Wit*. Cambridge, United Kingdom: Mainsail Press, 1991.

Holden, Anthony. *William Shakespeare: An Illustrated Biography*. Boston: Little Brown and Company, 2002.

_____. *William Shakespeare: The Man Behind the Genius*. New York: Little Brown and Company, 1999.

Honan, Park. *Shakespeare: A Life*. New York: Oxford University Press, 1998.

Kay, Dennis. *Shakespeare: His Life, Work, and Era*. New York: William Morrow, 1992.

Lambirth, Andrew. *William Shakespeare: A Biography with the Complete Sonnets*. London: Brockhampton Press, 1999.

Macrone, Michael. *Brush Up Your Shakespeare!* New York: Gramercy Books, 1998.

Nolen, Stephanie. *Shakespeare's Face: Unraveling the Legend and History of Shakespeare's Mysterious Portrait*. New York: Free Press, 2002.

Picard, Liza. *Elizabeth's London: Everyday Life in Elizabethan London*. New York: St. Martin's Press, 2003.

Quennell, Peter. *William Shakespeare: A Biography*. Cleveland, Ohio: World Publishing Company, 1963.

Wood, Michael. *Shakespeare*. New York: Basic Books, 2003.

On the Internet

Adams, Dr. Simon. "The Spanish Armada." http://www.bbc.co.uk/history/state/monarchs_leaders/adams_armada_01.shtml

Shakespeare: A Day at the Globe http://www.guidanceassociates.com/shakdayatglo.html

In Search of Shakespeare—William Marries Anne Hathaway, 1582. http://www.pbs.org/shakespeare/events/event92.html

Renaissance Drama. http://athena.cnglish.vt.edu/~jmooney/renmats/drama.htm

Brooke, Arthur. *Romeus and Juliet*. http://www.clicknotes.com/romeo/brooke/welcome.html

The Seven Ages of Shakespeare's Life. http://ise.uvic.ca/Library/SLTnoframes/life/lifesubj.html

Shakespeare's School—Stratford-Upon-Avon. http://www.likesnail.org.uk/

Shakespeare Oxford Society. http://www.shakespeare-oxford.com/

Henry Danvers—Biography. http://www.geocities.com/garydanvers/EoD-DNB.html

Wiltshire County Council—Wiltshire Community History. http://www.wiltshire.gov.uk/community/getprinted.php?id=333

Butler, Ellis Parker. "Shakespeare-Bacon Controversy Solved." http://www.ellisparkerbutler.info/epb/biblio.asp?id=2358

"Views on Shakespeare Through the Ages." http://www.bbc.co.uk/
education/asguru/english/08shakespeare/39biogandcontext/
shakecontext02.shtml

History of Doubts surrounding the authorship of Shakespeare's Works.
http://www.shakespeare-oxford.com/histdoub.htm

Much Ado About Something – Forum: What's at Stake? http://www.pbs.
org/wgbh/pages/frontline/shows/muchado/forum/

Baker, John. "The Case for the Christopher Marlowe's Authorship of the
Works attributed to William Shakespeare." http://www2.localaccess.
com/marlowe/pamphlet/pamphlet.htm

Lady Jane Grey. http://englishhistory.net/tudor/relative/janegrey.
html#Biography

Lady Jane Grey. http://www.ladyjanegrey.org/

William Shakespeare. http://www.allshakespeare.com/shakespeare-
masters/47542

Pepys, Samuel. *The Diary of Samuel Pepys* http://www.blackmask.com/
books24c/pepys.htm

Hartman, Carl. "Shopping for luxuries in Shakespeare's time—oh, for a
damasked pair of spurs!" The Associated Press, October 25, 2005.
http://seattletimes.nwsource.com/html/nationworld/2002581474_
shopping25..html

"Summary of Baconian Evidence for Shakespeare Authorship." http://www.
sirbacon.org/links/evidence.htm

Elizabethan Sports. http://www.elizabethan-era.org.uk/elizabethan-sports.
htm

Robinson, Bruce. "The Gunpowder Plot" http://www.bbc.co.uk/history/
state/monarchs_leaders/gunpowder_robinson_01.shtml

Gunpowder Plot Society. http://www.gunpowder-plot.org/gun-plot.htm

Forbes, Keith Archibald. "Admiral Sir George Somers colonized Bermuda for
Britain" http://www.bermuda-online.org/sirgeorgesomers.htm

Heidorn, Keith C. "The Weather Doctor Almanac 1999." http://www.
islandnet.com/~see/weather/almanac/arc_1999/alm99sep.htm

Kathman, David. "Dating *The Tempest*." http://shakespeareauthorship.com/
tempest.html

Vance, Dr. Laurence M. "A Brief History of the King James Bible."
http://www.av1611.org/kjv/kjvhist.html

English Bible History—Timeline of how we got the English Bible. http://www.greatsite.com/timeline-english-bible-history/

Best, Michael. "Married Life." *Shakespeare's Life and Times*. Internet Shakespeare Editions, University of Victoria: Victoria, BC, 2001–2005. http://ise.uvic.ca/Library/SLTnoframes/life/children.html

Wiant, Jenn. "Shakespeare's latest ghost writer is now purported to be Sir Henry Neville." The Associated Press, October 20, 2005. http://seattlepi.nwsource.com/theater/245149 shakespearedebate20.html

David Garrick's Life. http://www.lichfieldgarrick.com/site/scripts/module.php?webSectionID=16&webSubSectionID=8

The Man Who Made Stratford and Shakespeare Famous. http://www.sirbacon.org/links/dg.htm

Rao, Shailesh. "Tradition, Tourism, and a Town Hall: The Story of Garrick's Jubilee." http://nkorda.web.wesleyan.edu/myth/jubilee/garrick.html

Glossary

allusions (eh-LOO-zhuns) indirect hints referring to something else.

ardent (AR-dunt) especially strong feelings of support.

belligerent (beh-LIH-juh-runt) warlike, hostile.

bombast (BOM-bast) artifically inflated.

catechism (KAA-tuh-kih-zum) formal summary of religious beliefs, often in a question-and-answer format.

chamberlain (CHAYM-bur-lun) an important officer in the court of a king or queen.

consonant (KON-suh-nunt) in agreement.

copyright (KAH-pee-ryt) exclusive legal right to use and/or distribute something, such as a literary work or an invention.

dynastic (dye-NAH-stik) relating to a succession of kings or rulers in the same line of descent.

epic poem (EH-pik POH-um) a very long narrative poem featuring the adventures of an especially heroic figure.

erotic (ih-RAH-tik) referring to or arousing sexual desire.

liturgy (LIH-tur-jee) the form of rituals used in public worship.

mutton (MUH-tun) cooked meat from a full-grown sheep.

reconciled (REH-kun-syld) brought together; settled; resolved.

secular (SEH-kyoo-lur) having to do with worldly rather than religious matters.

soliloquy (suh-LIH-luh-kwee) speech given by an actor to himself or herself that reflects the character's inner feelings.

strident (STRY-dunt) harsh, insistent, often grating to the ears.

tankards (TAN-kurds) tall drinking containers with a handle; many have lids.

topical (TAH-pih-kul) having immediate interest, either in terms of time or location; directly related to the topic.

trestles (TREH-suls) forms with braces used to support something else.

triumvirate (try-UHM-vuh-rut) a group of three people, usually connected as rulers or leaders.

troupes (TROOPS) groups of actors or other people who perform regularly in a theater.

Index